TESTIMONI

I have had the pleasure of reading Kalifa's doctoral dissertation, working with Kalifa at a Fortune 500 company, working with Kalifa again at a tech startup, and now reading Kalifa's latest work: *I Think I Love My Job*. Kalifa is that rare human-resource talent who brings a mix of research science and the experience of a tested practitioner to a business conversation. This is a must read for business leaders and HR practitioners who have already done it—and may be doing a few things not quite right. For example, in chapter 2, Kalifa deconstructs the beloved and misapplied Employee Net Promoter Score. You'll read it and wonder why you didn't think of that. In chapter 11, Kalifa reframes diversity, equity, and inclusion in a thoughtful and compelling manner. Her take on DEI—informed by her lived experience at home and in the workplace—is timely given the current reexamination of DEI practices in corporate America. I think you'll walk away from this chapter with a pragmatic compass amidst the fog of rhetoric from all sides of what has become a hot political debate. Kalifa closes her book with a last chapter called "I Think I Love Solutions," and that is so her and so this book.

—**Minh Hua**
Chief People Officer, Omniva

I Think I Love My Job is not just a book; it's a road map. It is a call to action, empowering leaders to prioritize their most valuable asset: their people. I love how Dr. Kalifa Oliver masterfully intertwines academic insights, compelling storytelling, and actionable strategies to uncover the many ways a leader can use people-centered design to reshape their employee experience. If you're committed to building a workplace where every employee feels valued and inspired, this book is a must read. Prepare to be enlightened, inspired, and empowered to revolutionize your organization's employee experience and create a workplace where everyone truly loves what they do.

—**Ariel Belgrave**
Chief Wellness Officer & Board-Certified
Executive Wellness Coach, GymHooky

Dr. Kalifa Oliver offers a compelling and relatable exploration of the challenges inherent in each phase of the employee experience. *I Think I Love My Job* transcends the confines of HR departments and DEI teams, speaking to the entire organization. For anyone in a leadership role, this book is a must read (and I mean a read—pun intended). Dr. Oliver adeptly demonstrates the practical significance of the what, how, and why behind the employee experience, making this book essential reading for anyone tasked with shaping this journey within their company. I don't just think—I know: "I love this book." Highly recommend.

—**Solomon Bennett**
Consumer & Employee Research Leader

At a time when so many people and companies are thrashing out their approach to work and management, Kalifa Oliver delivers an essential, biting critique of the status quo with deep insights into how we can create truly meaningful and effective work environments. *I Think I Love My Job* is poised to launch the next wave of employee experience practice. Not to be missed!

—**Ben Waber**
Visiting Scientist, MIT Media Lab

I THINK
I LOVE MY JOB

I THINK
I LOVE MY JOB

Secrets to Designing a People-Centered
Employer Value Proposition
(That You Can Actually Boast About)

KALIFA OLIVER, PhD

press 49

Press 49
4980 South Alma School Road
Suite 2-493
Chandler, Arizona 85248

Volume pricing is available to bulk orders placed by corporations, associations, and others. For bulk order details and for media inquiries, please contact Press 49 at info@press49.com or 833.PRESS49 (833.773.7749).

FIRST EDITION

Library of Congress Control Number: 2023923457

ISBN: 978-1-953315-35-9 (paperback)
ISBN: 978-1-953315-37-3 (hardcover)
ISBN: 978-1-953315-36-6 (eBook)

BUS012000 BUSINESS & ECONOMICS/Careers/General

Cover design by Anna Bullock
Interior design by Medlar Publishing Solutions Pvt Ltd., India

Printed in the United States of America

This book is dedicated to:

*My parents, Trevor and Camlyn Oliver, who always instilled
in me the importance of treating everyone with kindness
and gave me a deep appreciation for ensuring that people
have a good experience, no matter their job.*

*My husband, James, for always having that kind
and loving patience with me and being my rock
and support at all times. Thank you with love, always.*

*My kids, James IV, Aria, and Annalise, for reteaching me
the beauty of discovery and reminding me to stop, slow down,
and enjoy both the little and big things—and that there
is always time for a belly laugh.*

*My sisters, Aisha and Malika, for always seeing me
as only me and for always being my refuge,
my safe place, my link to childhood, and my home.*

*In memory of Dr. Linda Rochelle Lane, who embraced me
unquestioningly like a daughter and who gave me a deeper
appreciation for being myself. Thank you for treating me
like your own and always challenging me to be my best self.
I miss you, and I hope I am making you proud.*

CONTENTS

INTRODUCTION

WHY THIS BOOK?

I began studying the employee experience academically before the construct even had a name. At the time, I was looking at it through the scope of industrial-organizational psychology, studying statistical modeling, with variables like employee satisfaction, commitment, organizational resources and constraints, engagement, stress, and burnout. But as I advanced in my career, I figured out that, in practice, all those concepts fell nicely into a whole new field centered around the employee experience.

I also accidently discovered an unexpected passion for data despite my absolute hatred for math. Maybe that makes me a bit nuts, but something about the ability to search for truth and understanding problems that people can't seem to get a handle on really drew me in. Problems that always felt intangible, based in constructs and theories, became tangible data and numbers that could be looked at scientifically. Then, I found that I could take that data and tell people's stories in a very concrete, yet practical and solution-oriented, way.

I wanted to learn more, but I mainly found either academic research or opinion pieces. It was harder than I expected to find really good data-driven advice that was also practical and actionable. As I furthered my career, did more consulting, and listened to countless employee voices through more formalized continuous listening programs, it occurred to me that I had a responsibility to create more data accessibility and democratizaton for the employee experience because it could help us all.

But I am also human.

I know that sounds like a strange thing to say. Incidentally, it also sounds suspiciously like something a robot would declare, but I digress. Even with the credibility of all of my academic qualifications and my wealth of professional experience, I also chose to write this book from a very human perspective. I have been an employee. I have been a leader. I have been a consultant. I have had to design employee listening, employee experience, and people analytics strategies from scratch. I have had the privilege of having a seat at the table, but I have also had to sit outside of the door. I have been on the receiving end of positive and negative employee experiences throughout my career, and as such, I have had the opportunity to experience work from all sides—the good, the bad, the ugly, and the completely diabolical—in ways that have indelibly informed my craft.

Let me share a bit of my story and some of my inspiration for writing this book.

I spent my entire life either going to school or working (or both). I had reached a point in my career trajectory where I was beginning to see the fruits of my labor and of my passion. One could say I did everything I was told to do academically and professionally in alignment with social, cultural, and financial norms. Then in March 2022, something unexpected happened. I jumped on a business video call to be shocked by my entire immediate family

(I'm talking my parents, siblings, husband, and kids) on the call alongside my manager and professional peers. Now, how every one of them managed to keep this secret from me still remains a mystery to this day. But they were there for the announcement of my surprise promotion to VP! I cannot begin to describe the euphoria of it all and of that moment. It was the best of times.

Four months later, that company laid me off. I felt like nothing more than a number to them and a failure to myself. It was the worst of times.

Logically, I knew better. I knew that it was not my fault, but I felt completely lost. As I took time to recover from the hit psychologically, I recognized that I had the gift of understanding the employee experience on my side to give me perspective, the ability to disassociate my identity from that job, and the renewed vigor to create better experiences for employees. With that realization, I began working on this book.

Four months later, I secured a new role in the middle of a tough job market. Seven months into that new role, I found myself laid off again.

But this time I did not let a career setback pull me backwards. I kept writing this book. And with each keyboard stroke, I ensured that this book would deliver a story, a message, and an understanding of how work can be better with greater focus on the person—the human—not just through what I cognitively know but also through the lens of my own personal experience of work combined with how I've experienced my own intersectionality. This is why I can confidently write in a comprehensive, informed way about concepts like employee engagement; workplace trauma; performance management; talent planning; and Diversity, Equity, and Inclusion (DEI). It's not just what I know and do; it's who I am. I genuinely believe that everyone deserves to have brilliant experiences at work, from the moment they apply to a job to the moment they exit that company. I hope the holistic, yet practical, perspective in which I have chosen to write this book shines through and brings some much-needed clarity.

This book will introduce you to the concept of a people-centered design, the method of breaking down policies, processes, and pipelines across the employee life cycle and at every stage of development or redevelopment of programs. A people-centered design ensures that you pause purposefully to consider carefully how each element of the design will impact the people likely affected by resulting organizational programs or systems. Throughout this book, I will use the people-centered design as a key framework to help enhance the understanding of the concepts introduced and to help you think through implementation and actions as you begin to construct brilliant employee-experience solutions for your organization.

I wrote this book as a resource for the leaders and professionals who have the vision and responsibility for creating brilliant end-to-end experiences for employees. This book is for the ones who are charged with executing an employee-experience strategy and are searching for the right framework and architecture to begin what can sometimes feel like a daunting, impossible, and often thankless journey of transformation. This book will help you gain a more conceptual understanding of the employee experience as a strategy and how to navigate its nuances. It will also help you execute your strategy and give you insights on the best ways to produce actionable results.

This book is here to help you define your work experience and support your efforts to describe and articulate your strategy. I am here to tell you that I understand the challenge of being in your position. You want to make changes and do the right thing, but it is not always easy or clear to understand what the right direction looks like from an overall employee perspective. It is not always easy to understand what people are trying to articulate to you in your organization, just as it is not always easy for the people in the organization to understand what you are trying to communicate to them.

For a long time, it felt like leaders and organizations were on one side and employees on the other, and for a lot of my career, I have felt like a conduit in the middle. But I eventually recognized an interesting point. Neither side understands that they are often saying similar things but speaking in different languages. Everybody identifies their ultimate goals differently; though, at the end of the day, when we sit down and really think about all the elements of organizations, their bottom lines, and the experiences and products being created, we find that we can all get to the same place. Even though goals and paths are different, there can still be overall alignment.

The employee experience doesn't have to be this intangible construct that no one can achieve because it isn't cost-effective or it's wishy-washy. It can be concrete and tangible and useful. It can pour back into the business just as much as the business pours back into its employees. That is what I want to share. Here is a resource and all my musings. Here are the most practical ways in which I can tell you about what the employee experience is and how it connects to what you are trying to achieve.

This book is for everybody who exists within the corporate organizational ecosystem.

I want leaders to read this book and walk away saying, "I think I know what I need to do and how I need to do it." I want the chief financial officer (CFO) to say, "These are practical solutions that we can afford to do and cannot afford to ignore. We need to make the investment in this additional product and recognize our employees as the customers of that product."

I want you, the average, everyday employee, to walk away saying, "I understand the elements of my job that make my work the experience that it is. I understand what I need to do as a member of this organization, which might even require not being a member of this organization anymore. I recognize my role and my responsibility as well as the role and responsibility of my organization."

I want everyone who reads this book to walk away with an understanding of what the employee experience is and how we can use data to enhance it. I want you to question the way we view concepts like loyalty, commitment, engagement, and satisfaction in the workplace. I want you to have the ability to identify workplace trauma and recognize that even though organizations have evolved into bastions of performance and productivity, they do not necessarily need to dominate every single second of life. You will walk away with the realization that work can be a complementary part of what you do, who you are, and what you are willing to identify with.

Dear reader, thank you for coming on this employee-experience journey with me. Whatever your role in your organization, I am here to be your resource and your Rosetta Stone. I am here to be practical. I am here to be me—the best person in the best way I know how. I am here to make you laugh. I am here to give you a new perspective. I am here to challenge your thinking. I am here to drive you to action. I am here to make a difference and help you think differently. I am here to help you wake up one day and say, "You know what? I think I love my job."

I THINK I LOVE THE EMPLOYEE EXPERIENCE

Once upon a time, I worked with a company where the leadership was determined to reverse remote working arrangements. They officially called it "footprint reduction." It was aimed, they said, at increasing engagement, productivity, and efficiency. While I understood it from the finance, real estate, and—let's call a spade a spade here—control perspectives, I debated up and down with my leaders over the engagement issue because the internal data clearly showed that their remote employees had higher engagement, that they had better overall employee experiences, and that their performance numbers appeared comparable to, if not better than, those working in the office. "We don't care," was the response I received (and I'm quoting directly there). "We need to reduce our footprint, and we need everybody in the office because that's where we're getting the most creativity and innovation." I continually warned them that the data was clearly telling a different story, but at the end of the day, what did I know? Their remote employees reported being generally happier with the flexibility of their work arrangement and having a healthier and more productive work experience. But my warnings were of no use. The leadership stubbornly refused to listen to me. And then came COVID-19.

From a healthy distance, I watched that company's leadership suddenly scramble to reverse all the policies they tried to implement against my recommendations. Full transparency: I watched, and I smiled, and I watched a little more and smiled a little more. It was a much-needed lesson in humility for these executives, who, besides not listening to me, had refused to listen to their employees and the employee voice through data. And, dear reader, I pettily enjoyed every single moment of it. Had they listened to me a year earlier, they would have been prepared for the incredible workplace changes that COVID-19 required. They could have successfully managed so many of those unanticipated variables. While they buried their heads in controlled forecasts, I was considering all the possible things and examining the data for upcoming trends. For these same companies, the employee experience was never a priority. Yet the onset of COVID-19 forced them to make it a priority because they could no longer afford to keep ignoring it.

The uncertainty of 2020 changed so much about the workplace environment, but nowhere was that change more obvious than with the employee experience. Every leader of every company that spent years crafting plans to enhance the employee experience was wrong. Every single one of them. While it's easy to blame the pandemic and all the uncertainties that came along with it, the real reason lies in the fact that you simply cannot predict the human experience. Yes, the pandemic threw in some unfamiliar variables, but the truth of the matter is that the human experience is always variable. Employees are human beings, and human beings must constantly deal with the shifts and fluctuations of life.

So, to sum it all up, these companies were wrong in 2020. The fantasy forecasting was wrong. The data was wrong. Did I say they were wrong? And guess what? There will be another point in time where their forecasting will be wrong again, and it looks like it may be sooner than most executives think.

We have moved into this new environment where we see executives talking about the future of work while rolling back so many of the policies they put in place. We are seeing increased layoffs as companies try to manipulate their numbers. But behind their games is a level of dehumanization that stems from living in a society in which work is such a large attribute of who you are. When companies take jobs away, they also pull the ground out from under their employees by seizing part of the identity that society had crafted for them. Companies want a return to the mindset where employees are only seen as numbers on a spreadsheet. But things are much different than they were in 2019, when most people felt powerless to push back. Now, we are seeing a fighting response, where employees demand better and are not afraid to walk away. They have started to realize that work is an experience and a part of their life. But it is not the totality of who they are.

But it's not just the employees who are pushing back now. It's also customers, business partners, suppliers, analysts, and consultants holding these companies accountable rather than simply blaming employees themselves. The response of many people who are observing changes in how companies are treating and exiting employees has evolved from "How did you get laid off?" to "How dare you do this to your workforce?" Many companies have demonstrated that the moment they have a struggle, they'll get rid of you first—as an initial part of their strategies rather than as a last resort. But the stigma of these impersonal actions is now viewed through the lens of organizational accountability, and it's beautiful to see.

The future of work has become a popular hashtag and the topic of countless LinkedIn posts. I find it funny, though, because the future of work is right now—and it's wrapped in the employee experience.

When companies are constantly thinking about the employee experience, when they are constantly thinking about people and doing people-centered design, the future won't sneak up on them.

WHAT IS THE EMPLOYEE EXPERIENCE?

Simply put, the employee experience is a measure of the sum of all the experiences employees have within an organization that are provided and maintained by the organization. It starts from the time a candidate submits an application to the time they finally walk out the door, be it an exit, a layoff, termination, or even retirement. Think of it in the same way you think about your health. Your overall well-being depends on a summary of multiple measures, like your weight, your height, your genetics, your cognitive functions, and much more.

Look at the employee experience in the same way. It is a sum of multiple different things, such as benefits, technology, and compensation. Companies and organizational decision makers should want to know that they are providing a good environment to work in and that they are providing their employees with the resources to be productive and to do work well. Anything within the control of the organization can be used to measure the employee experience. This is because the sole reason for looking at the employee experience is so that the organization can do something about it. That is a key point in this discussion. If a company is not truly willing to act on any deficiencies found with the employee experience, then it is not honestly invested. And if it is not invested, it is best not to bother pretending that it is.

Far too many executive leaders see the employee experience as something impractical, too steeped in science to be accessible. But guess what? Science does not have to be intimidating. The majority of people speaking in this space have never even looked at data, yet they call themselves experts and provide information that is either too academic or too loosey-goosey. The employee experience is neither. Yes, it is complex because people are complex, and it also covers different stages and phases. But when you know how to measure it and what data to analyze, measuring the employee experience becomes highly doable.

A good employee experience is quiet, like taking a vacation. When you have a great vacation, you do not think about it being a great vacation while you're on it. Instead, you are busy experiencing it and feeling all the warm fuzzies of a good time. It's only when somebody asks how your vacation went that you realize it was good. But when you're having a bad vacation, you experience the bad times in the moment. You are completely aware of how bad everything is. You missed the plane. Your flight was delayed. Your hotel is awful. You hurt your foot. You lost your wallet. You hated everything about your vacation, and every element of your vacation becomes salient to you in the moment because they're noisy. Bad experiences are noisy, and good experiences are quiet.

A lot of what I do around employee experience is not shiny. It's not pretty or sexy. But, like a vacation, it is quiet, and people only observe it when it doesn't exist.

THE RESPONSIBILITY OF THE EMPLOYEE EXPERIENCE

You want to know the biggest difference between executive leaders and toddlers? Toddlers ask more questions. Think about it. Every time you answer a toddler's question, you have to think ten steps ahead of them because countless more questions will soon be coming at you in rapid fire. And don't even think about using "because" as your answer. You have to break it down, speak in a specific way, and use language that they understand. You also have to be prepared because they will keep asking questions until your answer finally makes sense to them. We can learn a lot about communicating in this space from interacting with toddlers.

When I discuss data and analytics with a leader within the context of the employee experience, it's an entirely different experience than many people would expect. There are very few questions (if any at all) compared to what one might expect when critical decisions need to be made. If they don't understand the data shared, they generally will not tell me, even if it makes no sense to them at all. Leaders, too often, have been put in the uncomfortable and unfair position of having to pretend they know everything and have all the answers at all times. There is a social pressure on many executives to not ask too many questions lest they appear weak. In many cases, they also can't understand why it doesn't make sense. So, at times, they have no context about the right questions to ask. Before I have a discussion with leaders, I intentionally activate my lessons from talking to toddlers to ensure that what I discuss with them feels more practical and relevant to my executive audience. I focus on telling the story of the data and on the experience that the leaders are having with me in the moment. When I do that, I see the moment when any confusion or frustration leaves their faces as I start speaking in their language and using the context that works for them. So if I'm talking to a CFO, I'm talking about numbers in terms of money. If I'm speaking to the CEO, I'm talking about the bottom line or the overall impact on the company. Suddenly, there is a light that comes on when it all makes sense because all they want is the answer. They just want to know what to do.

Dear reader, I love business, I love organizations, I love leaders, I love executives, and I love efficiency. So rest assured that I don't mean any of this in an insulting way. It's just that a lot of business executives prefer to stick with what they are accustomed to. And that's okay, but that often comes across as a resistance to data. But data is not necessarily a strong suit for many people, and that's okay, too. You don't need to go read an academic journal on how to figure this out. You also don't have to hire an excruciatingly expensive, fancy consulting firm (cough cough) for help. Instead, I want to give you a practical way to apply data, analytics, and insights to improve the employee experience. As you read this, I want you to hear me in the room with you—your favorite friend and homegirl giving it to you real and holding your feet to the fire. I'll be in your ear asking the hard questions, like "So you're really going to ask everybody to come back to the office when you had no difference in productivity? Seriously? Is that what you really want to do? Why?"

I want to be your employee experience conscience, your people-centered inner voice. I tell every leader I work with that any time they design a new initiative, they should ask themselves, "If I add this program or implement this initiative, how will the target employees experience it?" They should also ask themselves:

- How would employees experience it if I make everybody come back to the office?
- How do people with disabilities or divergent abilities experience that?
- How do caretakers experience that?
- How does this decision actually impact the bottom line?

My life's work has always been leadership decision support. It's a balance between me as an expert in people analytics and data and as an expert in industrial-organizational psychology. I'll throw in some nerdiness because that's just me. Listen, if something is a bad idea and completely unsupported by real and validated evidence, I am going to tell you it's a bad idea. And if it's a good idea, I will tell you why and how it will likely work. I'm trying to get people to think differently. And I think it starts from the top with decision-makers.

Contrary to popular belief, the employee experience is not the sole responsibility of the chief human resources officer (CHRO, which is sometimes called the chief people officer [CPO]). The chief executive officer (CEO) needs this information. And the chief financial officer (CFO) especially needs this information because they are often the blocker or advocate of important experience investments. The chief operating officer (COO) needs this information because people are part of their operations whether they want to admit it or not. And I want the chief diversity officer (CDO) to have this information because if they design their experience well enough, really thinking about people as a whole, true diversity, equity, and inclusion (DEI) becomes a natural product of what they're doing.

WHY YOU NEED TO LOVE
THE EMPLOYEE EXPERIENCE

Every business has some type of offering it provides to earn revenue. Whether it is a service or a tangible product, companies must produce something that consumers are willing to pay for. But there is much more at stake. Consumers use the quality and value of these offerings to assess your company and decide whether they want to continue spending their money on your products and services. As a result, companies spend a lot of time and resources perfecting that offering and getting to its highest level of profitability. Think of how much is invested in customer research, product innovation, and product development. Companies go out and get better talent, better skills, better innovation, and better creativity. All these elements result in a better product and a more profitable pipeline, which incentivizes and creates more loyalty within their customer base.

Well, guess what? Your employee experience is also your product, and just like your tangible offerings, it impacts your organization's reputation. It is a product of the decisions your organization makes, whether you are listening, whether you are willing to hear what employees have to say, or whether you are amplifying your employees' voices and thinking intentionally about creating an ideal environment for someone to work in.

Getting the best productivity and the most highly engaged employees comes down to the experience your company provides. So, in a sense, your employees are another set of customers. And not investing in making the employee experience positive also impacts your bottom line—but in a different way. While it's easy to look at your ledger and see the immediate impact of customers who buy a specific offering from you or the financial impact of consumer spending on your shareholders, it may be more challenging to identify the long-term impact of this employee-experience product. If your company becomes known as one that provides an extremely miserable experience and hurts its employees, you are looking at things like lawsuits and reputational damage. You are also looking at customer loss, recognizing that some of the people who buy your marketed products are also your employees.

Today's companies are operating in an environment in which consumers care about the experience that companies provide their employees. Consumers do their homework and pay attention to news about layoffs and downsizing. They want to know how this experience impacts diversity or attrition and how, by extension, that can impact the quality and consistency of the product itself or the product support they will get if they choose you. I have seen and talked to people who have decided not to do business with specific companies based on their poor employee ratings. They are ready to cut and run because they recognize that the social impact you are having as an organization will eventually impact them personally.

It has come to a point where many organizations can no longer get away with the things they got away with in the past. Customers' increasing scrutiny of organizational business practices and the way they treat their employees is having greater impact on how these companies are viewed and how customers are willing to interact with them.

In the same way you pour energy into and invest in your products, consider how you can position your employee experience. If you reframe how you think about the employee experience and how you're providing it, seeing it as an actual product your organization offers to your community, your country, your environment, and the market you are in, then you can really understand the impact of the employee experience.

When it comes to customers, businesses have done this for years. They have personalized, optimized, and measured. They have told customer stories and pivoted when needed. They know how to do all of this because leaders see customers as people. After all, consumers fall on the correct side of their balance sheet: the profit side. But companies fail to recognize that their employees are their biggest brand ambassadors. They are the base of the brand value. Look at the tech industry, for example. Many of these companies crafted idealized public visions of what an employee experience can be, with fancy buildings, free meals, and seemingly relaxed or generous benefits or workplace policies. Yet when we peeled back those well-designed layers, we discovered that many of the companies' employees were incredibly dissatisfied with their work experience, and many of them didn't want to say it out loud for fear of not being believed or not going against the well-designed, external-facing corporate images. We figured out that a company put a bed in the office so employees could sleep there. They told employees to bring their pets and even provided childcare so that their employees never had a need to leave. These realizations have led to widespread backlash against these tech companies, and now we are even seeing many of them downsize as a result.

The increasingly public diminishing reputation, post-pandemic, of a popular social media platform also demonstrates the connection between the employee experience and brand value in real time. When leadership changes led people to question the treatment of employees, users and corporations began to leave the platform publicly and loudly. Not only was that company impacted, but other companies associated with the new leadership were also affected by extension. A collective sentiment grew, where fewer people wanted to work for any of the companies under such leadership. A façade broke. Leaders like those taking over this platform were previously able to say, "Oh well, it's no big deal. Somebody else will come along and want this job." But that doesn't seem to be quite the whole truth anymore—because the employee experience matters.

It's hilarious and yet also so sad (and frankly a bit annoying). Employees have always been valuable, but companies did not truly see them that way until 2020—when they were forced to do so. Employees began really thinking about their mortality, thinking about their health in ways that they hadn't thought about before. Thinking about their well-being in ways that they hadn't thought about before. Thinking about their relationship with work. They were at home and realizing that these companies would let them go in a heartbeat.

If there's one thing that 2020 should have taught executive leaders, it is that the employee experience is a big product and that those who really focus on that product are winning right now. They understand the importance of that additional product, that secret sauce other companies are now catching up with. It's not too late, though. It's not too late to pause and implement some tools to listen to, to understand, and to amplify the voices of your employees so that you can understand what's happening and start working on their employee experience. That is up to you. That is up to you as an organizational leader. That is up to you as an organization.

That is up to you as a human leading other humans.

CHAPTER 2

I THINK I LOVE EMPLOYEE ENGAGEMENT

I know some people have strong feelings about engagement. So please forgive me as I throw a few huge curveballs into some things that you believe to be the whole truth about this construct. First things first: the employee experience and employee engagement are not interchangeable. They are not the same. In fact, engagement is more in line with satisfaction, loyalty, and commitment, which are all side effects of the employee experience. Employee engagement focuses on factors that are implicit and within the control of the employee, such as their energy, their sentiment, how they're feeling, their thoughts, and how they are experiencing work. This differs from the outcome-driven factors of the employee experience.

Are you ready for the next curveball? Engagement and happiness are also not interchangeable. A lot of human resources (HR) professionals like to define engagement in terms of an employee's enthusiasm and morale, making the assertion that engaged employees equate lesser turnover. Companies have embraced this perspective and bought into the theory that happiness equates engagement, so they spend money and resources trying to create happiness with pizza, ice cream parties, and happy hours. But these efforts are in vain for a number of reasons. First, that type of temporary happiness is fleeting and totally subjective. Yes, one employee might enjoy having a slice of pizza with coworkers, but another might find this forced engagement off-putting and disruptive to their productivity. Second, employees often do not expect, and should not have to expect, to find joy at work as a default. They may instead find joy in their families, friends, hobbies, and pets. But that is not the goal of going to work each day. Now, if they happen to find it, that's great, but most do not. So why are you trying to force it? And what are you actually measuring?

When at work, employees simply want the resources they need to do their jobs productively. Besides, what value do you get from a person who is filled with joy but completely nonproductive? We all know that person. I like to call her Coffee Judy. She has a coffee cup permanently attached to her hand as she bounces from cubicle to cubicle, asking everyone about their weekends, their families, and their pets. Any subject will suffice. Coffee Judy spends her time annoying the employees who are there trying to do their work. But she is also very happy. She joyfully walks around the office doing nothing. Meanwhile, I am engaged but dissatisfied because Coffee Judy will not leave me alone. I am silently dying inside as I wish for just one leader to tell Coffee Judy to have a seat. So this whole idea of happiness is overvalued. It is not the key to high performance or employee engagement.

THE MOTIVATION CONTINUUM

Traditionally, employee engagement has been discussed relative to variables like satisfaction and commitment. That is because many surveys and measures of employee engagement, especially the most popular or well-marketed ones, tend to focus on satisfaction, commitment, and loyalty. But at its core, employee engagement is a more internal variable, closely tied to motivation.

Motivation exists on a continuum of autonomy. At one end of the spectrum lies extrinsic motivation, where you are solely motivated by something completely external to you. If that thing is taken away, you are no longer motivated. On the opposite end lies intrinsic motivation, which is the thing that you would do even if you didn't get paid and that you will continue to do if nobody was looking. A person can go from internally motivated to externally motivated and vice versa. So you are either really passionate about it, or you are doing it because of some external reward or exchange.

Nobody is intrinsically motivated to work because work happens in exchange for a salary or benefits. And no, I didn't misspeak. Also, don't @ me on my socials about this. There is no typo or error here. I'll say it again: nobody is intrinsically motivated to work because work happens in exchange for a salary or benefits. However, there are other points on the continuum that are most applicable to the workplace: identified and integrated motivation. The employee experience is the integrated side of the motivation continuum. Think of it this way: the motivation to work, in and of itself, is not usually likely when our livelihood and way of living doesn't depend on it. In other words, most of us probably wouldn't work if we didn't have to. We would spend our time pursuing passion projects, which is typically what you think about in terms of somebody being very internally or intrinsically motivated. I know what you're probably thinking, though. What about the person who turns their passion project into a business? After all, we are constantly being told that if we follow our passions, we will never work a day in our life. But studies show that when you invest money in or place a monetary value on a passion project, it becomes work and less motivating. You move from intrinsic to integrated to identified motivation, which is where engagement lies.

Identified motivation occurs when you identify with the tenets and values of the organization that you're working for. The motivation to work is sustaining, helping you to cope with existing factors that may prevent you from doing your work. The engagement brand of motivation is an employee's reaction to the job, their energy around doing the job, the little internal fire that drives them to get up and go to work every day. But let me be crystal clear. Employee engagement at its core should not be confused with employee satisfaction, commitment, or any of those types of variables. They're cousins. They might even be siblings, but they're not the same thing. Let's discuss why.

A SYMPTOM

As I discussed in the previous chapter, the employee experience focuses on the steps that an organization can take to ensure that employees are having an experience that is desirable and in alignment with the values of the company. It measures whether employees are able to do their work in a way where they can be productive and perform as highly as possible. That's the outcome both organizations and employees want. Employee engagement is more of a symptom that provides insight into the status of the employee experience. Think of it this way: When somebody's engaged in their job, they can sustain transformations, like mergers and acquisitions, a lack of resources, or other constraints. They have the coping mechanisms and energy needed to commit to the task and be good at it despite the obstacles. They tend to be more attuned to variables happening in the workplace and the constraints not allowing them to be as productive as they would like to be. They are sensitive to poor leadership and have the ability to see issues that others might not see because they are so attuned, aligned, and invested. However, it is entirely possible to be highly engaged but not committed to your organization. Let me give you an example.

Many people stay in their jobs solely because they love what they do. If you have ever talked to a nurse or a teacher, you will find that a lot of them find something special in the work they perform. They love the joy of caring for people or the act of teaching. They love what they do, and they would do it in another hospital or another school in a heartbeat if the conditions were a better fit.

Many researchers tend to equate engaged or highly engaged employees with less turnover. But think about this: if somebody is more attuned to all the positives and negatives happening within the organization, they will only sustain their coping mechanisms for so long. This is where the stress factor of engagement comes into play. Engagement can sustain some level of stress, which is really important in changing times like these and especially when dealing with something as unexpected as a pandemic. There have been such rapid changes to work as we knew it over the past few years due to the pandemic, including how we viewed and defined the entire work experience. The really engaged employees were able to initially sustain the changes, but there was also mental exhaustion and burnout that came along with that engagement. Think about when you are passionate about something. You are passionate about painting, but all of a sudden, you have a block in your vision. You are passionate about writing, but you have an insurmountable writer's block. No matter how much you want to create, it's not there, and the stress of trying only creates more stress.

Now think about your less-engaged employees. If you tell them that change is underway, they figure that they will just stay put and ride it out. You will not necessarily lose your less-engaged people, even when the organization isn't providing everything they need.

But you will lose your more-engaged people over time. That is why you must take care of engagement. An engaged worker can be creative and innovative to the point where they find ways to deal with things. However, at some point, that exhaustion and stress will take over. And when that happens, those highly-engaged employees that you take for granted on a daily basis will be done. You are going to either see a sharp decline in their performance or their ultimate exit from the organization. I have seen it many times, especially during the pandemic. Countless companies were shocked to find that they had lost many of their more-engaged employees, only to be left with the less-engaged employees who really didn't care as long as that paycheck cleared.

TAKING CARE OF ENGAGEMENT

Why is engagement an important variable for continuous consideration? When you have highly engaged folks and their engagement scores and measures start dropping, it's usually an indicator that something is wrong within your employee experience. And that is when you have to look at other experience variables. Companies invest a lot of money to determine their engagement scores. Yet they often cannot determine how this number relates to outcomes like attrition, turnover, and customer service. That is because their measurement of engagement is actually a measurement of commitment. As a leader, you are asking employees how much they like the company. You are asking about the company's reputation and whether an employee would recommend the company to friends and family. You fail to realize that you are asking about factors that don't necessarily get at the data you really want. You're conflating concepts, so you never really get what you're looking for. Yes, intention to leave is a strong predictor of actual turnover, but intention to leave is not necessarily a key indicator of whether somebody is engaged in a job or not because—news flash!—people could be highly engaged in a job and still want to leave. They like the job, but doing it has become stressful. That is what you should be considering when looking at engagement.

You start looking at your senior leadership, organizational reputation, and people managers. You start looking at all these other things in addition to engagement. Engagement is a symptom, and it's important to check it, much like taking your temperature to see if something is out of the ordinary in your health. Contrary to popular belief, it is not your answer to everything, but it is highly related to other things happening in your organization.

So, when doing an engagement survey, how much of a drop in engagement is considered a big drop? I get this question a lot, so let me give you the psychological answer.

It depends.

Sorry. I know that's not the answer you wanted, but it's the answer I have for you. It really does depend on a number of factors. For instance, how much of a drop is it? Is the drop happening among your highly engaged folks? Is it a big drop compared to other factors related to your employee experience? Which questions are you finding issues with?

I've seen a lot of companies make large financial or people decisions based on an engagement score, but how would you feel about a physician who made a life-or-death decision based on your temperature reading a little high? You would have some serious concerns, right? You would want a full workup to ensure that they understand everything going on with you. That way, when they start diagnosing and recommending, they are doing so in consideration of the whole person.

Engagement is a tool, and like anything related to people data, it needs to be contextualized. It is a data point, an indicator, a symptom that should not be considered within a vacuum. When you put your engagement surveys within a continuous listening program, you have a much richer dataset. But when you look at that engagement, you need to remember that it is not necessarily a key indicator of your turnover. Yes, it is related, but the more data you have and the richer the data, the better story you can tell and the better decisions you can make.

It is important to measure engagement, but it is just as important to make sure it's not a catchall for everything you want to know. If you want to know about satisfaction, it's okay to ask about it. If you want to know about commitment and loyalty, it's okay to ask about them. You don't have to name it *engagement* in order to get rich data from it. The more tools that you have in your tool belt, the more information you have and the richer your continuous listening program is. So please stop depending on this one tool.

One more point of order. Please stop using engagement as a punitive tool for performance. Simply because somebody is not performing doesn't necessarily mean that they don't want to. It could very well mean that they don't have the tools or resources they need, which is the fault of your organization. Again, engagement is one symptom, so before you go using it for punitive measures, make sure you get the entire picture.

THE eNPS MYTH

Remember those curveballs I warned you about at the start of this chapter? Well, here comes another one. When measuring employee engagement, a lot of companies like to utilize the Employee Net Promoter Score (eNPS), which has a ten-point scale (in theory) and measures how likely employees are to recommend their company to others as a positive place to work. The theory is that this information gives a useful indication of employee engagement, commitment, and overall enjoyment. It essentially takes the NPS scoring method, which is commonly used to determine customer satisfaction, and changes it to measure employee satisfaction. But I am here to tell you that friends do not let friends use the eNPS to measure engagement or employee experience, and here's why.

If I go into Target and I don't like how the employees treated me, I can walk across the street to Walmart or Aldi or Whole Foods. I have a lot of options and choices available to me, which makes the decision easier. I have immediate power here; in psychology, we call this a weak situation. But work is different because my livelihood depends on it, and I have less immediate power; it is a strong situation. If I work at Walmart and I don't like how I am being treated, I cannot just pack up my stuff and walk across the street to immediately start working at Target. In fact, they would probably call the police to come remove me. While you can easily patronize another business, you cannot as easily or simply move to another job. There is a lot more riding on your decision. So you cannot measure these two different situations using the same methodology.

The responses given to any eNPS question can depend on numerous contextual variables. Would you recommend the company to a friend? Well, it depends on which friend. Would you recommend the company to a family member? Well, that depends on which family member. During COVID-19, when people could not find jobs, workplace desirability had a pretty low bar. The answer to these questions also depends on the economic environment and a person's financial situation.

The eNPS is a ten-point scale on its face, but it is really just a three-point scale masquerading as a ten-point scale. The calculation of the scores splits the scale (and I want to add here that the odd splitting of the scale is another point of contention, but let's leave that alone for now), where nine through ten are considered promoters and one through six are considered detractors. All other middle numbers are not used in the calculation, so the ultimate scoring only consists of negative, positive, or neutral. From a statistical perspective, the eNPS is not the strongest measure of employee engagement; honestly, it's one of those well-marketed metrics I have yet to see validated for any real construct in scientific literature related to employees—and people have tried. It really is much closer (maybe) to a measure of organizational loyalty (if that). Yes, it is a value-added metric to use in understanding the full context of employees, but it should not be used as the key metric for organizational or performance evaluations. I tell my clients that I'm cool with their adding the eNPS to their tool kit of understanding the full spectrum of employee experience (heck, the more data, the better, right?). And this is only if they use the scale's full ten-point capacity and not its customer-centric calculation. But when they start using it to punish, promote, or pay employees, that's definitely my cue to leave.

CORRECTLY MEASURING THE EMPLOYEE EXPERIENCE

We can correctly measure employee experience and engagement in multiple ways, and I refer to them as signaling. The typical signal that we think about is the voice signal. We want people to tell us how they feel, and the easiest way to make that happen is to ask them. It's a self-generated report of their sentiment and feelings about what is happening within the workplace. Though it can be flawed, it is still a signal. Most companies do not properly utilize voice signals, though. They fail to ask the follow-up questions necessary to break down the elements of their employees' experience, which is also a deficiency of other engagement tools, such as the eNPS.

Then, there are movement signals, where you look at more objective employee movement toward, within, or away from the company. This is where people are telling you something with their feet. Are they drawn to your company and clamoring to get in (application rates)? Are they quickly accepting job offers (hire rates)? Are they staying with the company (retention rates)? Are they leaving at an unexpected rate (voluntary attrition/turnover rates)? Are internal candidates moving around within your company (internal transfer rates)? This last question could, for example, signal that they might not like their specific or current jobs (or a particular manager) but that your company has something they appreciate. You must pay attention to and monitor these critical movement signals.

There are also connection signals, where you analyze how people connect at work. For instance, not everybody who has the title of *leader* is an actual leader. We literally have influencers within organizations who people gravitate to for whatever reason. It could even be our good friend Coffee Judy. Everybody knows Coffee Judy because she has been to everyone's cubicle.

Connection signals can also be measured through organizational network analysis, which allows you to understand how people engage and interact with one another and evaluate how these networks are growing. LinkedIn uses a similar model, where it shows users which connections they have in common. Connection signals help you identify the strengths in your network as the people tell you who they value most. Maybe it is a person who you have not promoted, yet the findings show that everybody listens to what this person has to say. When there is a problem, everybody goes to this person for assistance, evidenced by the fact that their inbox is flooded with emails every single day. This person probably needs to be promoted because if you lose this person, you risk breaking your network. People help create invaluable experiences for other people within organizations, and exploring connection signals can help bring that to light.

The last type of signal is what I call click signals. Where are people going in the tools and technology that your company provides? Are they clicking around? Are they going straight to specific items or topics? Is the information being provided clear? Are they going to other websites? If you don't give people an opportunity to speak and voice their concerns, they'll find a way to get a voice. You don't want to do an employee survey? Well, be prepared to hear about your company on a third-party site, like Glassdoor or LinkedIn. And speaking of LinkedIn, sometimes if you want to know whether somebody is thinking about leaving your organization, look at their activity on LinkedIn. If it has surged with a new profile pic and regular posts, they might be on their way out! Click signals can provide really good clues as to what's happening in your organization and where your organization may need to improve the user experience and technological resources that impact the experiences employees have and how they give you feedback. Though it can sometimes feel counterintuitive, there is so much value in paying attention to those click signals.

Measuring your employee experience is about measuring many complex things, including your network size and network connections. It's about asking employees how they feel. Surely you have found a way to measure customer sentiment, but have you found a way to do the same for your own people? If not, maybe that's because you aren't seeing your people as an investment, rather only as an expense. Companies invest in their customers because they bring in income. But they fail to see that their employees are some of their biggest ambassadors, assets, and early warning systems. Let me give you a very real-world example. I go to a fast-food restaurant and the employee behind the counter warns me not to eat the meat. Am I ordering a double-decker hamburger? No! In fact, I am not eating there at all. And with much thanks to said employee!

Organizations also need to remember that their own employees (and those in their close orbit) often need to reconcile the discrepancy in the treatment they get (or see another employee get) as an employee versus as a customer. Many leaders tend to forget that employees can wear both hats, and this is especially true of customer service and retail jobs. Let's say this: If I see that your own employee never buys from you, I won't either. I'm just going to assume that they know something that I do not know . . . or want to know. So think about that, too, when you measure the employee experience. How are your employees' potential experiences as customers also impacting how they see themselves as employees and organizational ambassadors? How, then, do you also streamline these two experiences so that they speak to each other in a functional way? It's all about paying attention to those signals.

As a closing thought here, I encourage you to think through all the signals and what they can tell you about the employee experience that your organization provides. But above all, remember that measuring the employee experience is only as successful as the actions you take on your findings.

CHAPTER 3

I THINK I LOVE CULTURE

There is no denying that culture plays an important role in defining the employee experience, but the leadership view of company culture is often different than the personal experiences of employees. On many occasions, I have been able to directly observe the disconnect between how leaders view culture and how people who work in the day-to-day front line of a company view culture. These leaders think that their formal declaration or written statement about company culture magically evolves into the actual culture that people experience. But that is not how it works. You can say it, write it down, or scream it from the mountaintops, but if your actions and inputs do not match what you are saying, your declared "culture" does not actually exist. The employee experience of culture stems from what the organization puts into creating it, and words alone are simply not enough. Your value statement is not your culture. It will never be.

Though sometimes used interchangeably, organizational culture and employee experience are not the same thing. Yes, culture is related to the employee experience, as it serves as both a product of and a driver for how people experience work. Simply put, culture is an outcome of the employee experience—then, it feeds itself. It creates a thread that should run through the entire organization, including all divisions, departments, localities, and even countries. The culture thread underlies the values of the organization, how those values are put into action, how they are maintained, and, of course, how they are sustained.

SHAPING COMPANY CULTURE

Culture cannot just be shaped from the top. It starts at the bottom. It doesn't matter how many emails, logo stamps, or shareholder packets you use to define your company culture, it is a bottom-up process. Yes, leaders can design and advocate for culture from the top, but if the culture you so eloquently write about is not reflected in the day-to-day experiences of your employees, then all you have are empty ideas, theories, and constructs. You don't have a culture.

As a leader, how often do you think about the perspectives of your employees that show up and do their jobs each day? Do you ever consider how your managers are actually managing and disseminating information? How about the way your employees interact with clients and customers? These are some of the factors that define your company culture because the culture is reflected in the experiences that people are having every single day—from your employees to your customers.

Take remote work, for example. COVID-19 changed the game, forcing many company cultures to quickly evolve, as people realized that their mental health matters and that work did not have to be their whole lives. Traditionally, a lot of employees did not want to communicate their concerns to their employers, either because the leaders did not want to hear it or because employees were afraid of losing their paychecks. But I have seen firsthand how far, deep, and wide that gap can become, creating a workplace filled with toxicity and resentment. This is extremely dangerous to organizations, potentially destroying a positive reputation. It can also become a driving force in attracting the wrong people to an organization.

Far too many leaders believe that they have the best, most progressive culture ever. Yet their actions, along with the actions of their managers and employees, don't align with their perceptions . . . and in some unfortunate cases, their delusions. Stop trying to pretend that you can just declare a culture statement and that is what manifests. No! Your culture can be toxic or dysfunctional, whether you are willing to admit it or not, and you are not going to understand that or be able to fix it until you really listen to your people through every signal available to you.

CULTURE GONE WRONG

Culture is a delicate balance that can be quickly thrown off. Again, from a previously used example, take the reputational decline of one extremely popular social media platform. The leaders maintained a culture that was widely regarded as positive and even innovative by employees on the inside and users on the outside. Yet a widely publicized change in ownership resulted in a major decline of the organization's culture. Though the new leader loudly proclaimed that nothing had changed, the employee exits and complaints from insiders told a completely different story. It only took one person to come in and destroy a culture that had been highly regarded for years. So much effort was destroyed virtually overnight. The "good old days" experienced under one regime were vastly different from what workers were experiencing under new leadership. The culture broke. It didn't matter that nothing changed about the written culture because what people experienced changed dramatically.

However, it doesn't always take new leadership to destroy company culture—even toxic employees can disrupt the balance. When leaders allow toxic people to stay in place, they risk demolishing any positive culture that may exist. We've all heard problematic language, like "Yes, this person is toxic, but they are also a high performer." Well, that one high-performing person can destroy your culture, so I hope the sales are worth it. The hard truth is that toxic people thrive where toxicity thrives. So if they choose to stay in your organization, it's because they feel comfortable and empowered there. If your company culture was as positive and highly functioning as you claim it is, those toxic people would run for the hills. Progressive environments smother them, because they are filled with people who don't feed into their toxic foolishness. They don't feed into the bad behaviors. Instead, they stand up and push against these behaviors.

Culture is affected by what is rewarded, and if leadership keeps rewarding bad behavior, even unintentionally, that will define the company culture. As employees start to recognize what is rewarded, they will change their behavior accordingly, even if it negatively affects the organization as a whole. Let's take Late Larry, for example. Late Larry never arrives on time—not to work, not to meetings, not anywhere. And his arrival is always unapologetic and entitled. Yet Late Larry is never reprimanded for his constant lack of respect for others' time. In fact, his behavior is always ignored and dismissed because of his years of employment and seniority. What happens when other employees observe Late Larry's behavior and lack of accountability? They stop worrying about their own punctuality as well. Before you know it, tardiness has become a dysfunctional part of the company culture. Why? Because Late Larry was senior enough to know better, and it seemed like the company's blind eye was a reward for and an endorsement of his actions.

Monetary rewards are another good example. Companies often give bonuses based on production or sales numbers. But the question becomes this: if you are doing this many sales, what are you doing to reach that goal? Let's be real. Sometimes people cheat to get there, even if it hurts the client or customer. This is an especially real and problematic issue in sales organizations. In companies that are so focused on targets without accountability for context, unethical shortcuts become pervasive—especially if the target is handsomely rewarded—means to end be damned! Yet this behavior is being rewarded as a matter of policy, which creates a situation where counterproductive and negative behavior is promoted. Leaders have to be really careful with recognition to ensure that they are not rewarding, and therefore promoting, bad behavior as a driver of culture.

FINDING YOUR TRUE COMPANY CULTURE

As a leader, it can be hard to recognize and accept the disconnect between how you see your culture and what it looks like in reality. Maybe you have people in your ear telling you what you want to hear and reinforcing your (potentially misguided) beliefs. It might also be a situation in which you have no clue that your managers and employees routinely behave out of alignment with your desired culture. You might not know that the decisions made and words spoken by your frontline employees are highly problematic. Whatever the case, this lack of awareness can be damaging to your organization. As a leader, you can set your intentions for the culture, stating your ambition for what you want it to become and the actions to get there. But to actually manifest those sentiments into reality, the steps and actions must be pervasive enough to reach and touch everybody in your organization. If they aren't, you must take steps to correct that.

The first step is acknowledging how your employees actually experience your company culture. And if you don't know, that means you likely have not been listening (a topic we will discuss in the next chapter). You cannot only listen to yourself and other leaders. Instead, listen by paying attention to the following factors:

- What are your people managers doing?
- What are your individual contributors doing?
- What are your frontline workers doing?
- What are you telling your clients?
- Are people leaving the organization?
- Are employees using words that don't seem to align with your stated values?
- Do you see things within management that lie outside of your stated culture?

This is the reality of your employee experience and where your culture lies and thrives.

The next step is checking your own efforts to drive the company culture. Is your ideal culture constantly repeated in all your messaging? Every company email and communication should include language that says, "This is our company culture. This is our vision. These are our values."

But it's not all about the words. Are you living and acting in accordance with the culture you want to see? Your employees are not stupid, and they are always watching your actions. If you are doing things that fall outside the stated culture, they take notice. I always warn leaders to be aware of what they are saying to their people. I'm not talking about body language. I'm talking about the messages they send in doing something that runs contrary to the words they are saying. That is the message your people are taking in. That is how it works in everyday relationships, including those at work.

To be brutally honest, by the time most organizations recognize a problem in their culture, it is already too late. It has been there for a while and manifested to the detriment of the company. Now, much work is required in order to see a transformation. Fixing a culture takes a good bit of time. It takes investment, and sometimes it's hard to turn around. But commitment, true action, looking at your reward structures, listening continuously to your organization, and pivoting when necessary can really help with building a culture that positively impacts the employee experience.

STARTED FROM THE BOTTOM...

In short, organizational culture is what is happening at the front-line and direct-manager levels. That said, culture can be modeled or broken at the top levels of the organization. Culture relies on trust. And like trust, a broken culture takes a lot of focus, work, and intention to repair or rebuild.

Culture breaks one broken promise at a time and is built one sincere, ethical, and intentional action at a time. If your culture matters to you, then so does your employee experience.

CHAPTER 4

I THINK I LOVE LISTENING

Within many organizations, employee listening (and to be clear here, I'm not talking about spying or monitoring) is viewed as a "nice to have." Companies typically have human resources information systems (HRIS) in place that provide some objective personal data, and as a result, leaders often mistakenly believe that this is all the data they need. I have heard them say things like "We have some data, and we already know what's going on." Well, as your new trusted friend and employee-experience conscience, I am here to tell you that listening must be done in organizations—it is not an option. It never should have been an option. And if you did not learn that in 2020 . . . let's just say that it cannot be an option anymore. Employee listening must be a strategic priority. Leaders need to constantly hear what's going on within their organizations to make decisions quickly. Listening produces data that helps contextualize objectives and metrics. It gives you the power and ability to make more informed, data-driven, and empirically based decisions. When you make decisions solely based on your HRIS, you miss a huge opportunity for context.

Without the addition of details and color to your data, all you can make is a super-uninformed best guess.

Whether leaders want to believe it or not, employees are the backbone of any organization, and they must be prioritized as such. That was one of the biggest revelations of 2020. Seemingly overnight, employers realized the importance of their employees. And a lot of organizations obviously were not ready for any sort of change. Employees keep the doors open. They are the frontline people who make the quickest adjustments. If you fail to listen, you end up stumbling. And a lot of companies stumbled because, for them, listening was a choice. It wasn't an organizational priority utilizing a strategic method of collecting data. Even many of the companies that did have some kinds of employee listening systems in place were not using them. When the dumpster fire that was 2020 started, the companies with the most effective responses were also the most well informed. They were already working on their technologies, which enabled them to quickly protect the employees: their brain trust, their labor . . . the folks that apply mental and/or physical resources to keep the company's product or service available to the marketplace.

Many companies found out quickly that they did not have the technological capacity or the resources to tackle the kinds of unprecedented and massive shifts happening in the global workplace. So they decided that being in the office was more important than applying the resources to ensure flexibility, even though flexibility has long been cited as the future of work. They were caught unaware and learned hard lessons immediately.

Listening to your employees is as much a priority as listening to your customers, listening to your shareholders, and listening to your board. When you hear things from your employees, you can make agile and timely decisions. You can then quickly turn critical needs around and mitigate risks to stave off organizational fires. Listen to your employees—but not in a passive way. You need an active and efficient listening program that is staffed correctly. You need a robust data science and analytics team and a variety of different competencies, such as industrial-organizational psychology, communication, and design, so that you can get things done with quality and at speed.

LISTENING REQUIRES ACTION AND VULNERABILITY

One of the greatest misconceptions about collecting employee data is that it is solely employee led. But true (and successful) employee listening requires action from leadership, which is where most organizations fall short. Listening without action is just surveillance. You are only collecting intelligence. If you truly want to listen, you must be willing to take necessary action in response. Employee listening is not merely a function of HR or employee relations. Listening is also an operational function because it creates data on which the company can act. It impacts expenses, investments, marketing strategies, and recruitment analysis. It also affects the culture, which impacts the organizational reputation. These are all reasons why true listening must involve action that accurately reflects the data being conveyed.

A lot of companies also take for granted the value of acknowledging what employees have to say. It's the simple art of saying, "I hear you. I understand. I am listening. This is what you said." As a kid going to the store, I would listen sharply to my mother as she recited her grocery list to me in detail. Yet I almost always came back with at least one wrong item. She would ask for unsalted butter for baking, and I would bring back salted butter. I messed up the entire baking plan because I did not acknowledge what I heard and verify that I heard my mother correctly.

Employees feel devalued when they are not truly heard. For example, as companies create DEI initiatives, there are voices from underrepresented groups saying things like "We did not ask you to change the company logo for Black History Month. We are happy that you did and thank you. However, that is not what we asked you to provide. What we actually requested was funding for our employee resource or affinity groups to bring in speakers to lead some valuable conversations about creating institutional change. Instead of doing that, you changed the logo and walked away, patting yourself on the back. Nobody asked for that, and you are not listening to us." In the end, the assignment was not understood. These companies didn't listen and lost the plot . . . and the trust of their own employees.

It takes a level of vulnerability to accept this type of feedback. Egocentricity, like self-indulgence and hubris, cannot be a part of real transformation. As employees passively or actively share how they feel and how you can make their experience better, they expect your openness to the possibility of hearing some things you might not like to hear. Leaders are typically insulated from hard truths because people do not like to tick them off. There is a power dynamic at play that keeps leaders constantly protected from negative information about the organization. This is basically a communication barrier, and they are only hearing what they want to hear, which is highly ineffective.

Leaders have to step back and say, "Tell me about myself, my organization, and my culture. Tell me what I am doing well and what I can change." Then, they have to be willing to listen and determine what is viable and practical to act upon now or later. Leaders get lost in their feelings about the comments and feedback from their employees on social media platforms, but they need to perceive these resources as listening tools. Look at the data and see how it differs from what you believe your functions and culture to be.

If there is a huge misalignment, that is valuable data in and of itself. It means that your people are not willing to tell you their thoughts until they are long separated from your company.

Companies spend so much money listening to customers, sometimes to the point of stalking them. They do that because they recognize the value of personalization. But they do not actively invest in their employees because they do not see them as important. When you give people a chance to tell you something, you can hear some of the most creative and innovative ideas along with some big problems.

CONTINUOUS LISTENING

Continuous listening occurs when organizations gather feedback broadly in a frequent and systemic way to support leadership and business decisions. The overall aim is to improve the employee experience. By investing in a continuous listening program, companies signal that they understand their role in the employee experience and that they are committed to establishing tangible measures that lead to actions. As implied by the name, continuous means that it goes beyond the annual survey, which is typically what you find in most organizations. It acknowledges the employee life cycle, from recruitment to the time they exit the organization. Continuous listening seeks to understand the unique and diverse experiences of employees across demographics and life stages within an organization.

There is an implicit assumption with any continuous listening program that the employee experience is temporal and continuous, with major time points that impact somebody's experience within an organization. At the same time, underlying events and circumstances are continuously happening and also impacting the experience. Let's think about some of the things that organizations may measure in a continuous listening program.

When somebody walks into an organization, their onboarding and orientation is extremely critical, so you want to measure this experience with continuous listening. There are onboarding and orientation surveys that examine the classes they took and the training they received. These surveys look at whether these offerings were helpful and enjoyable. Technology is another subject for continuous listening. Are employees being provided with the technological resources and credentials they need? Companies may also conduct a monthly pulse survey to keep an eye on employee sentiment, or an annual survey, which is what you find in most organizations. There are also various types of exit surveys that are given before somebody leaves the organization, whether voluntarily, involuntarily, or due to retirement.

I will go into much more detail about surveys in another chapter, but the point I am making here is that there are many different employee experiences that can be monitored continuously, and when you group all of them together, your organization can create a strong and viable listening program. You may have an intranet where employees can leave comments or have discussions. By assessing that data, leaders can identify patterns or trends that they may be missing or overlooking. Leaders can also look at external resources, like Glassdoor, Blind, and Indeed, for a better understanding of how current and past employees feel about things related to your organization and what they are sharing externally. When you put all these things together, you have a wealth of information that is a continuous stream of robust data for more complex analysis and insights. You can create a clearer and more realistic picture of where your organization stands in terms of culture and the employee experience—whether you're doing a good job, what things need to be fixed, and if you need to pivot. The key is continuously listening to what is happening.

Something I want to make clear at this point is that continuous listening programs are not catchalls. They need to be strategic and capture things related to critical business outcomes, measuring things that really speak to the experience of your employees as well as what your leadership is willing to do about it. Continuous listening systems monitor key drivers of the employee experience, which are typically things like career development, commitment, satisfaction, compensation, benefits, leadership, and organizational reputation.

With continuous listening, organizations replace one massive survey with more frequent ones that take the employee pulse when needed. They pick samples representative of the entire employee population and ask them questions every so often. Think about driving a car with no gas gauge. You are driving while guessing how much fuel is in the car. When the car unexpectedly runs out of gas, you realize that your numbers were all wrong and now you are stuck on the side of the road in the middle of nowhere. But the addition of a simple gas gauge empowers you with the constant knowledge of how much gas you have in the car at all times. Continuous listening works in the same way, providing companies with a constant gauge on organizational health, whether something is not working, and whether you are making the right decisions. You have more data points to consider for a true understanding of what is happening in your organization. More data creates more context, and more context allows you to evaluate the culture better.

CREATING AN EFFECTIVE CONTINUOUS LISTENING SYSTEM

For any continuous listening program to be successful, it requires three things: openness, commitment, and action. I have already touched on openness, which is an organization's willingness to truly listen. Data collected in a continuous listening program tends to be both intuitive and counterintuitive, holding a mirror up to leaders and executives, with an unfiltered view of their organizational reputation. Oftentimes, the information and data are not what was expected, but they have to be open to it, which leads to commitment.

When organizational leaders don't care about the data they receive, listening just becomes an exercise in collecting surveys, which is frustrating to those who take them. In a future chapter, I will go into detail about survey fatigue, but it's worth a mention here. People would willingly take a hundred surveys if they knew some action would result. But if a company's listening program is collecting all this wonderfully robust decision-making data, and the company chooses to ignore it for whatever reason, employees will take notice. They are not fools, and they will develop negative feelings toward you and your program. Until your leadership moves toward openness, commitment, and action, your continuous listening program is going to be unsuccessful no matter how much time, money, and resources you throw behind it.

There are four key components to building a continuous listening program at your organization.

The first is a strong technology investment. I can't say this enough. Your technology must work. In order for people to utilize your tools and give you the information you need, technology must be accessible to and convenient for them. You cannot have them begging to give you information and making the process more frustrating. Technological systems must be fast, quick, and accessible. The worst thing you can do is set up a program in which your technology is freezing, is glitchy, or just doesn't work. Give serious consideration to choosing a survey platform, including the type of technology and whether you will use a vendor to help facilitate efficiency and to drive your strategy more effectively towards desired outcomes. Technology is often seen as secondary in a continuous listening program, though it can lead to the total failure of the system. So you really, really, really need to invest in your technology.

Second, your organization needs strong and strategic data analytics talent. You need to have data scientists and analysts who not only know how to analyze data but who also are comfortable with people data, specifically, and all the nuances, quirks, complexities, laws, and rules that come with it. You also want people who are familiar with reporting and using data tools like Tableau. With the right level of skill sets in place, you can promote dynamic reporting better. You should also ensure that you have access to subject-matter experts who really understand HR data. While a data engineer or data scientist can help you understand data and build datasets, it is crucial that they are familiar with people data and HR data to conceptualize it. I strongly recommend hiring or contracting people with backgrounds in subjects like industrial-organizational psychology (I promise I'm not biased), organizational behavior, sociology, economics, and/or HR management. You need professionals who really understand theory and background through data patterns and trends related to employees. You also want to think about people with business intelligence and data architecture backgrounds who can pull data to build structures and systems.

Another tip about your people and data analytics talent: many organizational leaders don't think about this, but you want someone or some people who have a background in communications. Data reporting can quickly become too technical for general consumption, making it harder to understand what is being said or proposed. The important parts, such as insights and solutions, can get lost in the minute details. A communications professional can transform the collected data into reports that are palatable and easy for leaders to understand, so they can use it effectively to make decisions.

The third component is one you have heard from me before, but I am saying it again. A successful continuous listening program needs sponsorship and advocacy from executive leaders. You need support from executive leaders within the HR department as well as executive sponsorship from the C-suite. If you don't have these things, you can't get any technology you need, you don't have access to the budgets you need, and you may not be able to hire the talent you need. These leaders need to advocate and model appropriate behavior for the leaders and managers subordinate to them. When faced with the data, not only can they advocate listening, but they can also advocate action.

The fourth and final component is organizational readiness. Your organization needs to be at a place where it is ready and open and willing to discuss the results, be transparent about the results, and discuss what it would take to make changes. Your organization needs to use the listening tools and program as a springboard for overall employee experience improvement and stability.

Organizations must commit the resources, including time, technology, and talent, for any listening program to function correctly. They must create the right tools, make sure the analysis is good, and ensure the reporting is effective.

MAKING CONTINUOUS LISTENING WORK

Continuous listening must include systems that measure all four signals multiple times. Think about a mega-sized retail store that employs hundreds of thousands of people. It is experiencing extremely high attrition rates, and leaders want to run a global survey to determine what's going on at the company. Let's say that the survey had a 90 percent response rate, which would appear successful on its face. But there is much more to the picture. By the time you have downloaded, categorized, and checked the data; built out the reports, transferred them to managers, and translated them; completed the executive overviews; and cascaded these overviews down to the stores, you are probably no longer talking to the same group of people that actually took the survey. You are making decisions and taking action for people who likely have already left the company.

There is a common listening problem we call the recency event in which an organizational event affects how people react and respond to a survey or listening tool. For example, perhaps there are high engagement rates immediately following the distribution of bonuses. Of course your engagement rates are high. Who isn't happy after getting a bonus? But let me offer an example of how misleading that data can be.

Imagine that you have a publicly traded company where bonuses are given out each March, and your data shows that March is the time of year when both retention and attrition are at their highest points. How can that be? Well, would you leave an organization before getting your bonus? Probably not, and most people would not either. But once those bonuses are handed out, the two-week notices start coming in. Two things are happening in the same month, but if the company is not listening properly, it will miss out on one of those recency events. If the bonus checks come out on March 20, the retention numbers probably look really good on the fifteenth. Conversely, if you only look at attrition every year on April 1, you will see low retention rates each time. As a leader, if you solely consider the data gathered on March 15 or April 1, you will spend an entire year making decisions based on inaccurate numbers. A much more effective approach would be looking at attrition rates on the first day of every month. Doing so would uncover both the increase and dip in retention, giving you a better idea of which months offer the best data on attrition and retention.

That is why I question companies that bring in consultants only once a year. Think about it this way: What if I ask you how you are feeling today and you answer that you are feeling fine? Does that one-word answer provide any insight for you to make better decisions? No, it does not. You need a more comprehensive view, and some consultant firms just don't provide that. Now, I know that a lot of these firms will not like what I am about to say, but I'm not trying to win any popularity contests here. If you are going to invest hundreds of thousands of dollars (often at a minimum!) to bring in large consultant firms to help you take action on employee experience and culture matters, it makes sense to have a designated person to evaluate your options and ask the hard questions you may not know to ask. It may be someone you already have on your team, or you may need to put aside the extra money to bring in a vendor advisor or vendor consultant. Whatever it takes, this step is vital for securing a tool that truly gets at your organization's DNA. Don't get cheap now. For example, if you are going to spend a million dollars to listen to your employees, assuming you don't have an expert on staff, you can pay an objective third party consultant $50,000 (on average) to help you through the vendor selection and monitoring process to ensure that you are protected and well covered in how you define your business requirements, contract negotiations, and contractual support. This partner will help you ensure that your organization is getting the complete data it needs to make truly meaningful changes that can stick in the long term and will work within its overall strategic business and bottom-line goals.

Allow me to address one more pet peeve when it comes to consulting firms. A lot of leaders are obsessed with benchmarking, but what good is it if you are a retail company benchmarking yourself against Google or a company of 5,000 employees benchmarking yourself against Amazon? Yes, you are a financial company in the same industry as other fintech companies, but benchmarking your organization against them simply will not work. You need different tools and expectations. You want to make sure that when you are evaluating an employee experience/continuous listening vendor, you are comprehensively assessing what they bring as a whole and are looking at things like privacy, flexibility, customization, and personalization. You want to make sure that you are not stuck with garbage for multiple years. The vendor has a good tool, a good platform, benchmarking . . . and they have been around since 1904. It all sounds sexy. But the world has changed a lot since 1904. In fact, the world has changed a lot in the last ten years, including the tools and accuracy of the data. Mixing old garbage in with good data makes nothing better, so let's stop with the benchmarking obsession.

LISTEN TO EMPLOYEES LIKE YOU LISTEN TO CUSTOMERS

Effective listening requires the infrastructure and investment to do it properly, but when it is done really well, it is great. It is the same thing you do for customers. It may feel harder when done for employees, but it really is not. People want structure. They like to be heard, and they will work within a structure as long as they feel involved and included. They do not want to leave jobs—it is neither enjoyable nor desirable despite any claims to reinforce the tired narratives perpetuating in the ether. They would love to stay with the same company for a long time, but they also realize that they have lives to live and bills to pay.

Like your investment in the employee experience, listening to your employees using data and people analytics is not an option. It is your not-so-secret weapon for elevating your employee experience and optimizing the support you provide to increase loyalty, engagement, and commitment within your organization. Continuous listening is the program that you can invest in to take your organization straight into the future and then maintain its place there among truly great companies to work for.

CHAPTER 5

I THINK I LOVE SURVEYS

As I speak to organizational leaders about the connection between the employee experience and listening, I often get asked for my opinion on surveys. Conducting surveys is one of the easiest and most efficient ways to collect a lot of data at one time from across your organization. But there is a lot of curiosity surrounding what the right questions are, what topics are really critical, and what's actually actionable for the organization. The other thing I find myself discussing with key leaders is how best to scale a survey and whether it is the best option to have a vendor-led process or an internally driven employee survey process. Then, of course, there is the big one: what to do with the survey data once the process is complete.

This chapter will walk you through some important considerations when conducting organizational employee surveys. I'll also give you my two cents about the misconception known as survey fatigue (hint: it is not a real thing).

THE DESIGN PROCESS

There are two main groups that are extremely important when designing any survey data-collection process: the people who are responding to the survey (the respondents) and the people who will analyze the data (the analysts).

THE RESPONDENT

First, you need to know your audience (or your expected respondents). You need to understand key background and demographic information about them, like their average educational levels, their roles and job types (think how you might frame questions differently to a desk worker than you would to a plant worker), and their languages, language levels, and industry lingo. You also need to know how much time they may realistically have to complete the survey (think about a retail worker versus someone working in a manufacturing plant versus someone sitting in an office). For example, if you're giving a survey to a group of frontline retail employees, you likely should calculate "time off floor" costs. That is, you should multiply the median salary of the employee group by the estimated average length of time to complete the survey. This cost can also be affected by season in terms of the cost incurred on the floor by removing people from this employee group off the floor, no matter how briefly. For example, taking retail employees off the floor to do a survey during Black Friday is more costly overall than taking them off the floor to do the same survey of the same length during the slower, early summer period. In such cases where you may need to target retail employees or it is critical to launch an employee survey during a peak/busy period, the survey likely needs to be shorter (or have a shorter completion time) due to the "time off floor" costs to the business.

THE ANALYST

On the other side of the survey process is the analyst (and in a lot of cases, the key analyst is the same person who designed the survey, which is the best-case scenario). The analyst is focused on the back end of the survey and the quality of the data that will come once respondents complete the survey. For example, questions arise, like will the data make sense, or once analyzed and reported, will the data meet the original intents of the organization and organizational needs? This means that the organization's leaders must be clear about what they want to know or what problems they are trying to solve. While surveys can uncover unexpected findings, the data should not be so far from organizational alignment that it cannot be processed into critical insights for the organization.

Here is the thing: a survey doesn't have to be tricky. It's not a test or an assessment that you will do for selection. It is just a means of collecting accurate information. A survey is also not a puzzle, so it must be clear and concise. Why are you using words like *stress* and *happiness* when you really mean *satisfaction*? Just ask about satisfaction. If you want to know how important something is versus the frequency of use, then ask how important it is. It's crucial that the survey design is unambiguous as well as aligned with real goals and with how you plan to report and analyze it.

I say all this to make a point that the strategy for producing reports, analytics, and insights should occur at the design stage, not when the data comes back. The analyst should be brought into the conversation when the survey has already been deployed. And one more thing to drive this home: if you choose to use a vendor, an internal analyst should be partnered with the vendor to ensure that the entire design of the listening tool is optimized from the very start. Remember, a garbage design means garbage data in and garbage data out.

CREATING ITEMS

Creating survey items may seem like an easy task (I mean, *anyone* can conduct a survey, right?). But a *good* survey—one that gets back clear, robust data and actionable insights—is not as easy. Many people who have underestimated the science and expertise behind building a good survey tool have banged their head on a table at least once when the data came back or when they were trying to present findings to leadership.

A strategic mistake that I see lots of organizations making is trying to design surveys by committee. Let me tell you this: designing a survey by committee is the fastest way to spiral into absolute chaos. Don't do it. Have key stakeholder discussions first, and take copious amounts of notes focused on what the business and leaders are trying to solve. Design a survey tool with a small core group (even if this is a vendor-led effort), then send it out for comment to stakeholders. Cap the number of questions, question types, and comment deadlines—and be firm on these. Finalize the draft, then send it to key approvers. Ensure that you have extra bandwidth or real estate for item additions (and deletions) and a few alternative items in your back pocket in case the approvers ask for changes. Then, move forward to your survey launch. This process will save you so much time, expenses, effort, headaches, arguments, and missed deadlines. Thank me later.

The thing about surveys is that you need to find balance. You need to make trade-offs. You need to keep it simple while keeping the survey complexity and integrity. The bottom line is you cannot please everyone. You need to have a point of view and be able to make the case for which items are selected, which scales, and why. You have to be able to say no—even to leaders and vendors—and suggest valid and data-driven alternatives and solutions. You also have to decide when to relent; sometimes a leader really wants something in the survey, and it may not be helpful, but if you have the space and it is also not *harmful*, you make the trade-off. You also need to think about the time to complete the survey, scalability, global use, and translatability to both languages and cultures. You will always be tempted to ask about everything under the sun that you want to know, but you need to boil it down to what you *need* to know right now and within the relevant context of time for the process at hand. And you need to ask all of this in as few questions as possible and in the clearest way possible. (Whew . . . tired yet? Yes? Good. That means you are getting it!)

And now some other practical item-design tips to help ensure that you are creating a useful tool:

- No matter how much two things might seem related, you should ask them as two separate questions. For instance, if a baker wants to know if their cake is rich and moist, they need to either ask two separate questions or decide which characteristic is more important and only ask about that one.
- Double-barreled and double-negative questions can be confusing. Ask one thing at a time, and be consistent with phrasing. Avoid writing negatively worded questions (your analyst will thank you).
- Don't keep switching up what you're asking and how you're asking it. The first question starts with "I never . . ." The second question starts with "I have . . ." And the third question goes back to "I never . . ." again. I have observed this type of wording in many surveys, but it leaves too much room for error, potentially messing up the resulting data, not to mention that it often thoroughly confuses the respondent.

ITEM SCALES

Another critical survey consideration is scale. You must be careful about what scale you're using and ensure that it matches the item. For example, most sentiment surveys use the agreement scale, with responses ranging from "strongly agree" to "strongly disagree." But I've seen examples of organizations using this scale to gauge frequency, which makes absolutely no sense. I also want to note that your scale doesn't have to be a ten-point scale. If a five-point scale will do, use it. Unless you have a statistical reason for using it, a ten-point scale really isn't necessary. Sometimes you might use it because it's the typical format for your respondents, and you want to keep it because it's familiar or for consistency. Remember, while scale calculations can be recalibrated by the analyst on the back end, you want to design the items to align with both the items and scales as simply and as much as possible to minimize confusion and error.

You also want to be careful not to keep reversing, negating, or changing your item scales throughout the survey, which can create room for all types of errors for both the respondent and the analyst. Try to keep all the items that have similar scales together and only change the scale when absolutely necessary. You want your respondents to use as little cognitive energy as possible when focusing on your format and as much cognitive energy as possible when answering your questions candidly. Too much of a cognitive load creates frustration and can cause the respondent to quit or leave you with bad data.

ABOUT OPEN-TEXT QUESTIONS

I want to emphasize the importance of asking open-text questions. (Confession: unstructured data can be so annoying, but, nerdily, it is my absolute favorite kind of data. It can be so rich and robust. It can be such a labyrinth to explore and a puzzle to solve. I love it! Okay, back to the discussion now.) The qualitative data that comes from open-text questions usually provides much more insight into what is truly happening within your organization and allows you to expand the confines of your own personal bias. I strongly recommend open-text questions but with a serious caveat. If you have no intention of doing anything with the open-text questions, don't ask them. It takes a lot of time and cognitive energy for somebody to think about and write their responses, so they expect you to do something with it. This data could use natural language processing modeling or a thematic or sentiment analysis. There's so much you can do with this type of robust data, and if you choose to do nothing, you are missing out on a valuable opportunity to listen to your people.

A big consideration with open-text questions is privacy. When deciding whether to have open-text questions, remember that you are creating a space where people can share crucial, vulnerable, and, yes, horrible things. You have to work with your organization's legal and privacy teams (or, in some cases, external consultants who focus on these areas) to ensure that you have a disclaimer noting who can view verbatim answers and at what level of detail. While a survey can be anonymous or confidential, information contained in open text can break anonymity and confidentiality or may be a serious allegation that may trigger an employee relations investigation. Setting up the survey with these legal risks in mind from the beginning is critical to organizational trust and well-being. If the risk supersedes the ability of the organization to act, then open-text questions should be removed from a survey until processes are in place to protect all parties involved in the company. In addition, open-text responses should *never* be presented to managers, leaders, and executives verbatim. They should be scanned and masked through analytics, and these stakeholders should only be able to see the summary theme and sentiment analyses of open-text data, with select examples. This reduces the risk of retaliation and of breaking any legal privacy rules and laws. I know, many leaders demand to see the actual responses verbatim. Here is the reality: these should only be accessible to the select group of analysts within people analytics or general data analytics teams (and analysts who work for the vendor where relevant). Information about who has this level of access should be disclosed clearly up front to the respondents so that they can make informed decisions on what they choose to share. I'll talk a bit more about privacy and ethical considerations later on in this chapter.

RESPONSE RATES

I often get asked, "So what is a good response rate?" And I jokingly say, "Any response rate is a good response rate." But you should hope to get about 30 percent. That's a good rule of thumb for representativeness and where you can breathe more comfortably when trying to make an impactful decision. The truth is that a lot of small corporate surveys and pulses typically get 10–15 percent response rates (20 percent if you are fancy), which is not bad. The resulting data is usable, especially when they're not high-stakes surveys. But for big surveys with heavy investment, like annual engagement surveys and exit surveys, you often find 90 percent response rates. In many cases, it's due to high pressure, which is also not great for data quality. As another rule of thumb, these high-investment surveys should aim for 50–75 percent response rates. You want good data, not just data for the sake of having it. High-quality data makes high-quality decisions. Period.

However, I do want to stress that you shouldn't spend a lot of time trying to figure out why people did not take your survey. You can't figure it out because there is not a homogeneous reason. A lack of responses could be as simple as forgetting or as complex as a lack of trust, a fear of retaliation, or a protest against your organization. If, for some reason, you are very concerned about response rates, I recommend speaking with the nonresponders if you have a confidential survey format (and if this confidentiality is properly disclosed) to try to understand why they didn't respond. You could also supplement your survey efforts with other employee listening strategies.

ETHICS AND CONFIDENTIALITY

When designing, carrying out, or even thinking about a listening program, confidentiality is extremely important. Respondents answer a survey with a sense of vulnerability, expecting their input to be valued and respected (or in the very least *heard*), especially when there are open-text comments. You have to be extremely careful about how your organization treats such data and controls who has access to it. In my experience, most employees who take company surveys go in with the mindset that their responses are being monitored by management with the intent of retaliation for any criticism or negative feedback. Ninety-nine percent of the time this is obviously not true, but the nature of the employer-employee relationship and its implicit balance of power create that fear. And employees are constantly looking for evidence that their fears are justified—it's just where we are in the construct of work and how work has been traditionally designed. My advice to organizational leaders is to accept mistrust as a reality but *always prove it wrong*.

Here is the reality: you can get sensitive, serious, and stark responses in surveys, especially when there are open-text options. These responses can range from deeply personal to outright ethical and legal employment violations, including troubling issues like discrimination, harassment, abuse, misappropriation of funds, criminal behavior, and violence. Something that many leaders do not realize is that once someone writes down (or in some way reports) these kinds of things, the company cannot deny knowledge and may have an obligation to refer that data or those allegations to the employee relations team. They may also need to refer cases to the legal department to investigate problematic situations or issues involving higher-level leaders. Anything that comes through a survey can be information for an audit or a discovery in a lawsuit, which is why it is extremely important to ensure that critical stakeholders are included in the design phase of your survey/listening process. These roles include decision-makers in legal, risk, privacy, communication, and country manager (or similar) roles. It is of the utmost importance to flesh out and clarify disclosure up front for respondents. It is important to weigh the risk of open-text questions with the value of the data for key decisions. Your respondents should always be afforded the choice to provide their answers in a way in which they understand the potential impact and outcomes, especially when they choose to use a survey as a reporting tool. While we know that this is not the role of organizational surveys, this is often how they are used, and in many ways, employees see surveys as the only real outlet for them to be heard. Do not, under any circumstance, create a fuzzy area with trust, ethics, and legality when it comes to surveys and listening programs. The potential ramifications involve too high of a risk and are too dire, and the recovery process is much slower than the time it will take to ensure that your tool is designed well up front.

ANONYMOUS VERSUS CONFIDENTIAL

I cannot stress this enough: be clear on the differences between anonymous and confidential. These concepts are not interchangeable.

And please don't go by what a vendor may tell you because I have seen major vendors get this terribly wrong on multiple occasions. Anonymous surveys cannot be traced back to an individual, whereas data collected in an identified or confidential survey can be linked back to a specific respondent or key respondent characteristics that are embedded and do not need to be self-reported. Even if you ask respondents in an anonymous survey to self-report their own demographics, you cannot verify or validate it. People can lie easily or even take the survey multiple times, as it is an open link. Identified or confidential surveys can be completed only once or have to be cleared at the row level by a survey owner for it to be retaken by a respondent. This data is keyed and can be matched to an individual on the back end.

Anonymous and confidential surveys have pros and cons. How and when they are used is usually based on a matter of organizational need or intention. If you want a general understanding of or want to take a pulse on the culture, or if you need quick data to make lower-risk decisions, anonymous surveys are fine. You just need aggregate data to get an overall look at what is happening and a temperature check of the organizational environment. Anonymous surveys are good for a new leader or new team assimilations during transition periods for program or process feedback, especially new programs or processes, and for test-and-learn periods. Note: the major issues with anonymous surveys are that the data cannot be validated, respondents can take the survey multiple times, there is a much higher risk of respondents lying, and there is a much higher level of trolling in open-text comments. Basically, the data that comes out is much more likely to be messy. The positive aspect of anonymous surveys is that respondents may feel more comfortable being honest and you may get higher response rates (but you cannot truly validate that each response is a unique individual).

Confidential surveys are recommended for strategic decisions throughout critical organizational transformations because they allow leaders to make more high-impact strategic decisions and high-value/high-risk financial decisions. Confidential surveys allow for more precision and the collection of more robust data. Note: the major issues with confidential surveys are more rooted in potential privacy violations and respondents' fears of misuse, abuse, and retaliation by the organization. In addition, these fears often encourage employees to answer less extremely and less honestly, creating more inaccurate data. Organizations worry that they will get (and they sometimes do get) lower response rates due to employees being uncomfortable with responding.

Confidential demographic or personally identifiable data that can be linked to confidential survey data can be pseudonymized, meaning that even the analysts cannot see who the individual responder is. However, even with pseudonymized row-level data, there has to be someone in the organization with a key, meaning that the data is never truly anonymous. Data that comes from a confidential survey should only be reported aggregately and only seen by a few people at the row level, like the team of analysts and perhaps a vendor. It should never, ever be seen by a people manager or a leader (outside of the directly responsible analytics and reporting team). It has to be protected at all costs.

Confusing the two things—confidential and anonymous—can lead to heavy fines for privacy violations and massive cultural harm due to the loss of trust within the organization. The fines are generally imposed per instance, per person who receives the survey (they do not have to take it), if the survey is found in violation of global, regional, or local privacy laws and rules. So every time you send a survey invitation or reminder out, each individual email that gets it wrong is a fine. Bottom line: These fines rack up fast and can be retroactive. They can and should be avoided.

The truth is that with due diligence, duty of care, and a people-centered design of process, policies, and pipelines, much of the risks associated with confidential surveys can be mitigated, and the impact and data quality can greatly outweigh the risks. Organizations need to be aware of where they are in their culture, cultural trust levels, or at what stage they are on their employee listening journey. If you are at the beginning and want to establish a listening program, it may be best to start anonymously and go from there as you build trust. If you need to make high-risk or high-impact decisions, it is best to go the confidential route while giving yourself adequate time to ensure that your privacy plan and post-survey action strategy are laid out well. Regardless of what survey type you use, doing nothing with the data further erodes organizational trust and makes the whole survey and listening process a complete waste of time.

This brings us to survey fatigue . . .

SURVEY FATIGUE

In the world of surveys and measurement, something I hear a lot at all levels of organizations is the notion of survey fatigue. You hear it in academia. You hear it in marketing. You hear it within the employee relations and HR space. I'm here to tell you that **survey fatigue is not a real thing.**

Let me break down the idea of survey fatigue here. As it goes, if you send too many surveys in a short period of time to anyone, people (employees or not) get really tired of doing them. This then affects the response rates of all your surveys, so you don't get the best data available. But here is the dirty little secret every leader needs to know. Are you ready? They are not sick of your surveys. They are sick of *you*.

I know that's harsh, but let me explain. When people fill out a survey, it's almost like they're making a contract with you. They think, "I am providing you with this information based on my perspective with the expectation that something is going to come out of it that is tangible enough for me to at least see or notice at some point." These people want to be seen, heard, and valued, so they take their time and cognitive energy to give you the feedback that you are asking them for. The closer in time the action is to the collection (and reporting) of the survey data, the more likely people are to see the connection between the two. As a result, if you were to send another survey right after the action, that would reinforce their decision to participate. Thus, they are more likely to fill out the next survey that comes along.

When leaders tell me that they are worried about survey fatigue, I typically tell them that it's not survey fatigue. It's *inaction fatigue*. People are tired of your asking for their information, their time, and their cognitive energy just for you to send it into the void and do nothing about it. That's what they're tired of. You and your inaction. They are being offered what looks like a chance to have a voice, and they are speaking up, but they don't think that voice is being heard or listened to in any real way. So why bother? Nobody enjoys their time being wasted.

Think about it this way. If you are in any sort of relationship and your counterpart asks you to share your thoughts, feelings, and observations so your relationship can be improved but then no decisions made seems to ever consider your perspective, what do you do the next time they ask? Absolutely nothing. What's the point, right? You remain quiet and keep going about your business. And that is exactly what happens in organizations. When your employee grows quiet, don't use survey fatigue to shirk responsibility or to avoid the organizational reality—your problem is much bigger than people not wanting to fill out a survey.

The value of organizational surveys increases with action related to the outcome of the survey. It increases the most when there is at least a relatively clear connection between the outcome and what was asked in the survey. And believe it or not, discussing the aggregate or overall survey results in a formal or informal setting can be a good starting point. When you do this, your people feel seen and heard. They appreciate your recognition of the time they took to complete the survey and the value you place on their opinions.

Another way to mitigate this concept of survey fatigue (which as we now know is actually inaction fatigue) is to communicate the reason behind the survey. People are constantly trying to decide what to do with the all the things vying for their attention, their cognitive energy, and their time. Communicating the purpose of the survey, what it means, and the potential outcomes helps to create a shortcut for people to place a value on the survey based on their expectation and understanding of it *and its outcomes*. This creates more trust. Again, and this cannot be stated enough, you have to act on these outcomes to maintain the trust.

Bottom line: the failure of people to respond to your survey is less about the survey or even the number of surveys that they've gotten. People will fill out a hundred surveys back-to-back when they're being paid for it or if they see some kind of outcome that aligns with them and their own needs, even if that need is simply to be seen and heard. People would fill out a hundred surveys if they knew something of value was going to come of their participation.

I'm here to tell you that the concept of survey fatigue is completely overblown because the fatigue stems from your organization's inaction. Don't ask for my opinion if you don't care about it. If your drive is only performative or a check-the-box exercise, don't get mad when people treat you and your survey as such. If you don't truly care, they won't truly care. Be respectful of your respondents, and commit to what you plan to do with their voices. Recognize that people are taking time to tell you things that are sometimes difficult for them to communicate. And if you don't find a way to listen to them and act on it, they will find an avenue to share how they feel anyway (think Glassdoor, LinkedIn, Indeed, Reddit, and Blind, to name a few).

So if we ever work together and you ask me about survey fatigue, know that I'm going to sigh, roll my eyes, and say that it is overblown. Then, I'm going to ask you what you plan to do with the data. If you don't plan to do anything, your problem is not survey fatigue. It's your inaction. Period.

REPORTING

This brings up another important point. If you're looking at team-level data and reporting back to the team, you should always be aware of the number of responses sent back to the team leadership. My recommendation is that if a team has less than five responses, managers should not receive reports because you are opening a door for identification of an individual, which is not something that you want to do. This is also true when you have demographic cuts and breakdowns; the number should reset by the number of people who have responded in that segment, not by the number of people who have responded overall in that team.

Another key consideration of reporting is how to analyze open-text (unstructured) data is the use of more advanced modeling for open-text questions. A lot of organizations focus on using word searches to locate words and phrases within verbatim text responses that they have identified as critical issues, like discrimination or harassment. They use the presence of these words to decide whether to escalate the responses to relevant parties, such as the employee relations team. However, it is critical that organizations move with the times and use more advanced and emerging technologies, such as natural language processing and machine learning, which can more accurately identify trends and patterns in unstructured data. This allows for sentiment and thematic analysis, predictive analytics, and prioritization so that you can also identify things that go beyond your scope, understanding, and expertise to better identify sustained and emerging issues or trends happening in the organization. Using newer and emerging technologies also allows you to ensure that your own biases are not baked into the analytics processes or the design of subsequent tools or products.

The crucial responsibility of the survey analyst cannot be overstated. Once data is collected, the analyst has an obligation to report it exactly as it is. Data should always guide your decisions, not the other way around. You should not be trying to tailor the report to meet any preconceived standard or keep a leader from getting mad. Data should not be manipulated because it doesn't sound like something that you think is correct or that a leader will think is correct. Analysts have an obligation to report the data as it is. The data needs to drive the story, and sometimes that creates discomfort. But as an analyst or a data scientist, as somebody who's responsible for a continuous listening program, it is imperative that you stick to the true integrity of the data. Otherwise, your program is just a show. And if you plan to have a show, take that to Netflix.

Analysts also have an obligation to report any data breaches, including vendor breaches, as soon as they happen, which is necessary for maintaining trust. A major part of a successful continuous listening program, as well as any survey, assessment, or listening function, is trust. You get the most data when there is trust. And if the trust has eroded, if that trust is lost, your program will not succeed. It will not function correctly, and you might as well not have it.

Data is powerful. Data is very powerful. When you're looking at people data, always remember that every data point is tied to an actual human being and that there are real life consequences to any decision made using that data. You hold a lot of power in your hands when you build a continuous listening program, which means you also hold quite a bit of responsibility to both the organization and the employees. So it's important to be ethical, cautious, and accountable. It's important to recognize that you have a responsibility to every single person who comes into contact with your program and every stakeholder related to or impacted by this program.

Continuous listening programs are formidable and amazing tools that can have extreme powers for good if designed correctly, executed correctly, and used correctly. It is exciting when I see a continuous listening program working to empower employees and impacting the employee experience in a positive way while simultaneously helping organizations actively meet people, cultural, and financial goals.

ENHANCING THE EMPLOYEE EXPERIENCE THROUGH SURVEYS

Organizations can greatly impact the employee experience by listening through surveys, but this needs to be done correctly. I want to reiterate that surveys are a form of voice listening and are not the only ways to listen to your employees. But they do have the advantage of being more quickly distributed among wider audiences through multiple modes (technology devices, online, or paper), easier to collect, and faster to process and analyze. Listen, I can confidently say that I can create a survey like nobody's business. And I can do that because I think about both the respondents and the analysts. I also think about the stakeholders, privacy, and business outcomes at the design stage. From the creation of a survey to the actions that follow, respect for the respondents must be the center of the journey. If you consistently give consideration for the time and cognitive energy respondents use to provide you with valuable data, and you always keep in mind that every data point is an actual human being, you can create an environment in which your employees appreciate and even, dare I say, love surveys.

CHAPTER 6

I THINK I LOVE PEOPLE DATA

DATA AND THE EMPLOYEE EXPERIENCE

A major part of my career has been spent using data to help organizations improve their HR technology, HR process, and overall people experience. Organizations recognize the value of people analytics and data; they show this all the time in how they invest in the customer experience and marketing. The shift to focus more on selecting people data for employees and using this data in meaningful ways is slow, but it is emerging on the HR and talent side of businesses—but not without doubters and resistance, as it's often hard to calculate the return on investment (ROI) of employee investments in the short term.

People analytics is still an emerging field, but it is a powerful one that helps key stakeholders move data from reporting to insights and insights to stories. The power of people analytics and the power of people data are unmatched in bettering executive decision-making and building cultures and employer value propositions (EVPs) that are sustainable over time and throughout transformations. People data and everything we glean from it is the key to how we craft and continuously improve the employee experience.

TO SURVEY OR NOT TO SURVEY

When consulting with a client or partner, they often tell me they need a survey, and my first response (with a bit of side-eye) is, "Do you, though?" It is vital to understand the differences between the various methods for collecting data and what you actually need. It's also important to understand the types and formats of questions asked. First, let's talk about when to use a survey versus a focus group or some other type of research method.

When trying to get specific information from a lot of people, and fast, a survey is your best bet. It allows for a greater reach and quick feedback. It's also easier to analyze and report on. However, in some cases, you are trying to make a decision that is nuanced and complex, so it requires more information than a survey can provide. For example, you need more color, more adjectives, and more descriptors when you are trying to design your vision or your values. When you are really trying to dig into an idea or a concept, that is where a focus group or another type of research method is more useful than just a survey. Additionally, when you are asking a small group of people about something specific and you only want feedback, a survey is completely fine. But if you want to know employee feelings about culture and their reaction to leadership, a focus group is the right answer.

Focus groups are not the easy option, though. They are more labor intensive, and proper facilitation requires training to avoid the loudest person dominating the conversation. The person who's willing to say the most or speak first is usually a person who guides the entire direction of a focus group. You also need to consider whether multiple focus groups are necessary to get the information you're seeking. If it's a situation where you are trying to understand technical or process-driven subjects, you want to make sure that you're asking people of different skill levels. You also want to include people who have been at the company for different amounts of time. A secret that a lot of people don't think about (because it's counterintuitive) is that if you're trying to understand a process, somebody who is new to the job is usually the best person to ask. The person who's been there a long time with the most experience has often trained their brain to take shortcuts. So they can't necessarily describe every little thing they do. While you do want their feedback and expertise, you also need a nice mix of people for an effective focus group.

Focus groups require a lot more energy from participants and a lot more time commitment. They even cost your business more because you're taking time away from people doing their day-to-day jobs to be in the focus group, and it's important enough to do that. But if you are going to have a focus group, you need to commit to why you're doing it and what you want its outcomes to be. Be very, very clear about what your goals are, what your needs are, and what you're trying to find out and then do something with what you learn.

There is another way to collect data from multiple people that might give you some more perspective, especially when you don't have a lot of time and you need to collect a lot of information, and quickly, and that is using open-text questions. But there are some things to keep in mind. Open-text questions increase the time it takes for recipients to complete the survey. You typically don't want to ask a whole bunch of these questions unless it's absolutely necessary. If you find it necessary to include more than four or five open-text questions on a survey, a focus group may be the better option.

I usually recommend only one open-text question because it is not easy to analyze the resulting data. It's qualitative, and as rich and robust as it is, it is not simple to report on, which translates to a longer reporting time frame. Open-text questions also need to be specific yet broad. Let me explain. Have you ever been asked a question like, "Do you have anything more that you'd like to share?" Well, you could respond to that by saying anything, whether relevant to the survey or not. If you are looking for specific information, the open-text questions should be specific to that topic. Here are some examples:

- Is there anything else that you would like to share with us about leadership?
- Is there anything else that you would like to share with us about your experience at this organization?
- Is there anything else you would like to share with us about how you use technology that is more directed?

These questions are broad enough not to lead or prime the person answering towards a specific response, and open-text questions allow respondents to provide more information than they could with a close-ended question. Yet they are specific enough to focus the answer on one topic.

Open-text questions offer rich and robust additional data. They also inform changes that can be made to close-ended assessment tools and survey questions down the line. But if you don't intend to do anything with the open-text data, like making some sort of decision or escalating concerns to leadership, don't use them. People take that open text box seriously, and you have an obligation once you put it there to do something with it. So bear all of that in mind when deciding to use open-text questions.

Close-ended questions are the ones we tend to be more familiar with: "How do you feel about X? Strongly agree to strongly disagree" or "How likely are you to refer your friends or family to X? Zero to ten." They are specific, clear questions with a scale. You fill it out, and you close it out. Bing, bang, boom. It's also faster from an analytical perspective, especially if the scale is consistent throughout the survey. Close-ended questions are the most typical off-the-shelf listening tools and your fastest option.

When trying to collect and understand information, there's not always one single direction to take. For example, you can ask close-ended questions and then find that there are strange patterns. The next time, you might throw in an open-text question to see if you capture anything else. There may be a situation where you ask an open-text question and find some interesting things that you really want to dig into. So you conduct some subsequent focus groups as a result.

MISSING DATA

Organizational leaders tend to place an emphasis on response rates, which is fair because you want to make sure that data reflects a representative sample. But when people decide to put their cognitive energy toward something other than your listening tools, you end up with poor response rates and missing data.

So what does missing data mean? In short, nothing. Leave that missing data alone! You don't have it and there could be many reasons why, but don't make big inferences as to why that data is missing. You can make some educated guesses and look at trend data to get an idea of what might have happened. But from a statistical and factual perspective, you just don't know. Stop trying to place value on what you don't know.

Data could be missing from people for any number of reasons. Maybe your employees missed a communication about participating. Maybe they forgot about the communication they received weeks ago. Maybe they were actually so busy doing their jobs that the communication didn't register as highly important on their long to-do lists. Maybe they just hate you and the organization, so they ignored the communication as their way of protesting. Maybe they went through the entire process and forgot to submit their responses at the end. Missing data can mean so many different things, so stop trying to make these value propositions for why it is missing. It is ultimately more of a future or an additional research question than it is something to hang your hat on in the meantime.

The other reason I advise against focusing on missing data is related to the group of people who took their time and energy and used their attention to participate. Focus your attention on what they said instead of pining over the people who decided, for whatever reason, not to participate. I have seen so many organizational leaders and organizations make this mistake. They're so focused on why people didn't take the survey or participate in the focus group that they almost dismiss the people who did. Then, they use the missing data as an excuse for inaction. That kind of rationale sparks a chain of events where some of those people who were participating will eventually move into your missing data column—because you never bothered to focus on them when they provided you with data.

If your response rate is too low, then try again. Maybe you need to extend the time for the survey. Maybe you conducted the survey or held the focus group at a bad time. Maybe you need to figure out how to get some of the people on your front line to answer. Maybe you are using the wrong method by choosing a survey or a focus group. It is easy to assume that the amount of missing data provides some insight. But in reality, it might, or it might not. And when it comes to listening and statistics, "it might" means absolutely nothing. Now, in statistics, we could look at missing data when we're doing advanced modeling, but that is very different from missing data as it relates to the response rate. Missing data is just that . . . missing. Don't assign a value to it.

CHAPTER 7

I THINK I LOVE DATA STORYTELLING

When I was younger, I entered a lot of storytelling competitions. Though I had one main rival who always beat me, I was actually really good. I liked the idea of being able to paint a picture for somebody and help them see what jumped off pages for me. Combining my love of stories and storytelling with my passion for data and all things employee experience was a match made in my nerd heaven. But why would you want to tell stories with data anyway? Seems childish? I know . . . it sounds a little iffy, but storytelling allows the audience to hear and understand what you are trying to convey, especially when it comes to data that is extremely technical. It provides more insight than just a bunch of numbers and descriptors. So let's dive into data and the story it tells about what is going on within the organization and what leadership needs to know.

THE VALUE OF DATA STORYTELLING

While the idea of combining data to help us understand and improve HR systems is not necessarily new, it is still at a foundational stage compared to other types of people data, such as data that examines the customer experience. People data is dynamic. It changes often because people are so wonderfully (and annoyingly) unpredictable. The story must be adapted to what's happening in the moment. Storytelling with data starts with insights. It moves away from just simply describing what information was found. For example, you have a dataset in your HR data that shows an attrition rate of 20 percent and an engagement score of 50 percent. But those are just numbers describing what you found. Insights take it to another level by examining how those findings connect to each another and your audience.

You're not just talking about dollars and objects. Each data point is a human, and each human has a story that is impacted by every decision you make for that data point. Data should not exist in a void without context. Storytelling makes it much more relatable and less intimidating. It becomes easier to digest and more translatable into action for HR, C-suite, and business unit leaders who are not necessarily comfortable with these types of facts and figures. People data can feel different, so storytelling helps to paint the picture in a way that draws decision-makers in instead of making them lean away.

Stories generally have a beginning, a middle, and an end. And in many cases, there's also a moral or something that the story is trying to say or teach. There is an action it encourages people to take. When thinking about HR storytelling with data, there should also be a bias to take action (e.g., I'm telling you all this and showing you all this data for this reason). Otherwise, you are not storytelling or providing insight. All you are doing is reporting, and anybody can do that, right? You can get anybody to produce something with a bunch of numbers and hand it out, but without insight, that is not effective. You are not helping, and you are not getting to that stage where you spark conversation and encourage clear actions toward the next step.

Storytelling is supposed to extend the mind to envision what you're trying to say or do. This is what good storytelling does—it draws the audience in and surrounds them. Great data storytellers take the attention and focus away from themselves and toward what the data is saying. I know that sounds strange, but that's the magic that happens. If more of the focus is on you than on the data, then you are, once again, only presenting and not storytelling.

Effective storytelling requires you to think ahead of your audience. As kids, we were constantly being exposed to all kinds of books. To make that happen, an author intentionally thought about what kids might want to know. What are the lessons they might want to know about travel, letters, and colors? How do we put that into a story? How do we make this something that is relatable and engaging? That is what effective storytelling is about. You think about what your HR leaders, your C-suite leaders, and your business unit leaders want to know so that you focus on them when you're looking at the data. That focus also means using appropriate business jargon. Whether you are talking to leaders in finance, communications, legal, product, engineering, HR, sales, or data science (to name a few), you want to make sure that *your* language fits *their* expertise. You also want to think about what's top of mind for the business. You can try to be as effective as you want and use every single point in this book, but if it's not top of mind for the business, it's not effective because you didn't think of your audience ahead of time. Rule number one of data storytelling: *know thy audience.*

Data reporting and presentations tend to lean toward technical language. And I get it—you are smart and want to show it. But you need to keep it conversational. Make sure that what you are discussing (including the actual data points) feels salient, clear, and accessible so that people don't interpret it incorrectly. Instead of using the word *mean*, use *on average*. This phrase is more conversational. The word *significant* in data terms means statistically significant. Make that clearer with words like *meaningful* or *relevant*. When you talk about a normal or skewed distribution and central tendency, for example, use words like *negative*, *positive*, and *average*. It's about reframing the way that you present data to leaders—because a lot of people, including those leaders, will not ask for clarity for fear of sounding and feeling stupid. Data can be intimidating to even the most learned, so as a rule, always make the language straightforward and listener friendly. Remember, if you cannot explain it simply, then you do not understand it.

Again, never, ever, ever, ever, ever, ever, ever forget that the first rule of data storytelling is to know your audience. You want to know exactly who you're presenting to and what is relevant to them. Then, you can stay two steps ahead. Thank me later when the questions come.

THE AUDIENCE EXPERIENCE

I have an essential message for the leaders, as well as the analysts, who tell the data stories, so pay close attention. When sharing your data outcomes, it is not about you! Let that sink in for a second. It is not about you! It is about the audience experience.

Effective data storytelling has insight and visualization that brings the data to life. Whether you are using static reporting, like a PDF or a written report, or dynamic reporting, which might look like a dashboard where the recipient can play with the numbers to see outcome variations, the visuals should help the audience to make sense of your data. Help them create shortcuts in their minds to understand what you're trying to say. Tech-heavy data can be intimidating for some people, and you don't want to make your audience's eyes glaze over every time you show up in the office or virtual meeting or when they get an email from you. You're essentially asking people to use their cognitive resources to comprehend the data you're presenting. So bring it to life for them with storytelling. Take the gathered insights and weave them together in a practical and actionable way so that people feel comfortable asking questions and participating in a robust discussion.

I often joke that a lot of leaders and executives are like toddlers but don't ask as many questions. They also sign paychecks, so remember that, too. Think in advance about the things that may be important to those leaders or executives, and the different ways to share those things with them. Think about what the data is saying vertically and horizontally, across businesses and across people, so you can ensure that your insights fall in the right place. Solutions or potential actions should be highlighted, with evidence that exemplifies why they fit within the course of your data and insights story. A good data storyteller pulls people in and makes them feel okay, even when providing negative information. The best data storytellers' voices remain in the room (where it happens), even when they themselves are long gone.

Whether you are handing out a report or creating a dynamic dashboard presentation, you must think about the experience of the audience. If they click this, what does it look like? Does it get messy? Can they understand it? Could it be interpreted in multiple different ways? Can it be misinterpreted? You want to think ahead and understand carefully, test assumptions, and talk to your audience. Ask them what they need, and then create the presentation and story of your data that gets your message across in the most effective way.

Here's another nugget of advice: use culturally relevant visuals and graphics. Take Diversity, Equity, and Inclusion (DEI), for example. In most contexts, it is very America-centric, but that can ignore the cultures of other countries. Even within America, every region has subtle differences in what appeals to an audience, so be wary of those nuances. You may even do the same presentation and tweak it for different cultures, especially if you're part of a multinational or global company. Also, be as neutral as possible with language while still providing clarity and understanding. You don't want your point to be lost because you are using terminology or graphics that might be deemed offensive or demonstrate a lack of consideration for a specific person, culture, or diversity group.

And don't forget about the color scheme. It may seem like a minor detail, but some companies are rigid about the use of their business colors, so make sure that you select the correct color scheme. Manage the white spaces as well, and only include necessary wording that promotes a presentation that is clean and clear enough to draw the reader into the visuals and the insights that you're delivering. Data storytelling is a bit of art mixed with science. A room full of stakeholders can take what you have written, created, and designed and see the entire data story. A good data storyteller becomes a partner who can be relied upon as part of the solution, which is crucial to HR and talent analytics.

THE BOTTOM LINE OF DATA STORYTELLING

I'm sure you can tell by now that data storytelling is a whole experience in and of itself. And it, in turn, can be used to bring employee perspectives and their experiences to life in a way that creates a vision and drives action in a way that feels both realistic and practical and is cost-effective for the business. These last few chapters have talked about organizational listening, surveys, data, reporting, and insights—and storytelling brings it all together and makes it salient.

Improving the employee experience is usually one good data story away.

CHAPTER 8

I THINK I LOVE THE CANDIDATE EXPERIENCE

What does the candidate experience have to do with the employee experience? Here is the thing—the employee life cycle begins the minute someone applies for a job at a company. Think about it: from the moment a person completes an application to your organization, they are protected by numerous laws. You now have to retain their information for a legally protected amount of time and keep all of your notes. You have a legal obligation to protect their private and personal information. And lest we forget, they might have grounds to sue you for discrimination if they are not hired—and they might win. For all intents and purposes, once somebody applies to your organization, their experience begins. While not all candidates will become employees of your organization, all the people in your organization were once candidates. Your organization's actions at the start of someone's tenure, even before they are officially part of your organization, can have a huge impact on how they see the organization downstream. And to be clear, how a candidate views a company is crucial, even if they never join your organization as an employee.

IMPROVING THE CANDIDATE EXPERIENCE

There are several things your organization can do on a practical level to improve the candidate experience. First, be as human as possible. I've probably beaten, and will continue to beat, this poor dead horse through this book—brace yourself. By all means, understanding and executing on the value of automation in making the candidate experience more efficient is extremely beneficial, but candidates also appreciate some level of personalization. Many applicants, and those who eventually convert into official job candidates, see how they experience an organization's selection process as a realistic preview of the treatment they will receive throughout their entire employee life cycle should they be offered the opportunity to join the fold. And this is where seemingly simple things matter, like how recruiters and hiring managers interact and communicate with candidates. Look, I get that things happen internally after a role gets posted that can create complications for the experience you might have intended to offer to candidates. A big culprit of these situations are organizational transformations, where job budgets disappear, the scope of a job changes, or a posted role is nixed from existing at all. Whatever the cause, it should not be the concern of the candidate; though, organizations still have a duty of care to those who took the time to go through their application process. And frankly, the further along they are in the process, the greater the duty of care to that candidate. Just as it should go without saying that there is an urgent need to maintain respect for your employees, the same applies to candidates. Everything that your organization does, from the moment someone applies, contributes to the candidate's impression of your company. So, while you are directly interviewing them, they are also interviewing you, as they should regardless of whether there is a conscious attempt to do so. Your organization might be the best organization on the planet, the company that everybody wants to work for, but it does not give you the right to mistreat your candidates. Period.

What often goes unsaid is the fact that once these candidates do get into organizations, they don't necessarily forget how they were treated during the candidate process, and while they may try to fall into the culture of the organization and team, the experience they had at the beginning stays with them. Every negative work experience that follows reminds them of the initial treatment they received, and they wonder in quiet moments if they missed or ignored all the red flags during the hiring process. And sometimes the opposite is true. I can tell you that the absolute worst employee experience I have ever had, to date, was at a company that withheld the truth about its organizational aims and financial positions, gaslit me about the absolute chaotic and toxic environment that it had fostered, used my expertise to save face performatively and drive the company forward with its people strategy, then unceremoniously dropped me with a piss-poor "we just don't see this work as a priority anymore." But this was also the organization where I had one of the best, if not *the best*, candidate experiences that I have ever had. And it was that candidate experience that kept me hopeful and going, even as I quickly started to realize what I had gotten myself into. It helped me push through and cope with the absolute chaos. I'm also certain that there have been some who have experienced the worst candidate experience and then managed to find that the actual employee experience was much better. But that incongruence tends to keep people on high alert, waiting for the other shoe to drop, and that never allows them to be able to fully embrace the culture in the way an organization may intend.

Here is the thing that I want to be clear on, and this is why the candidate experience is important on its own but also needs to be firmly embedded within your employee-experience strategy: because the mismatch between your candidate experience and your employee experience has no real, good outcome. Even if it turns out that it was just a more isolated candidate experience due to whatever internal factors were at play, it doesn't matter. People will remember, people will talk, and people will spend time constantly trying to align their experiences to help them make sense. As a form of self-protection, people tend to connect negative experiences to each other so that they can avoid the potential impact that those experiences can have on their physical and mental well-being.

CANDIDATES AND CUSTOMERS

A key thing that I want to point out is that organizations should never be so arrogant that they believe that these candidates are not in an empowered position to be your customers, too. Your organizational reputation carries through on multiple social and public forums. The discussion about your organization can become harmful if enough people have the same negative candidate experience. This is made even worse if the employee-experience feedback is just as bad. Remember when I said to be respectful to your candidates? If you have a situation in which you declined a candidate with a generic note, fifteen minutes after they applied (something that I actually hear about a lot), and then you email them about completing your candidate experience survey, they will likely be pretty annoyed. What do you think will happen next? Or the other fun one that I see is when organizations mistreat candidates during the selection process and then have the audacity to subscribe them to a newsletter to keep up with the company in an attempt to promote the company's EVP marketing strategy. You cannot make this up! Many technologies used in selection systems are designed to help create all manners of efficiencies and process improvements. Let's say that your company has a long application process (because you *know* when your system is not optimized!), and someone takes the time to fill out the application. You can easily code an acceptable and respectful window of time for rejection if an applicant does not meet a critical minimum qualification for the role they applied to. So perhaps, just perhaps, they don't need to receive a rejection two seconds after they hit send. Right? Candidate-experience systems and processes need to assume that applicants are applying in good faith, even if it turns out not to be the case. Minimally unqualified applicants will be screened out anyway, so why not just take the time to give a thought to the human experience at the other end of your process? It's not that hard, and it does not take that much effort. People-centered design, anyone?

Your candidate experience is often seen by external people as a reflection of the employee experience. Your recruiters, those who source talent, and your schedulers are seen as your brand ambassadors, even though that's not their exact role. Your recruiters and talent acquisition professionals are organizational doulas and serve as the face of, and the critical introduction to, the reality of your company and what your company is purporting to offer should the candidate join as an employee. Make sure that your systems, policies, processes, and personnel reflect the values and the culture that you are trying to look for in your candidates. Ensure that candidates are not treated as commodities that can be arrogantly "kept warm" in a pipeline. Maintain transparency in your process—and see the human. Take the time to evaluate the roles being posted, and fix the job description. Let me say this again here: *fix the job description*. A lack of role clarity and its close sibling, the mismatch between the job description of the role and the actual role, are two of the main reasons for increased talent turnover within the first twelve months of hire. And can we take a minute to talk about these job titles? A lot of organizations have started getting creative with job titles, but be careful not to cross the line from creative into deceptive. If you are hiring somebody under the job title of director, but the job is really an entry-level position, then name it as such—it's not a director role. "Head of" is probably one of the worst offenders in the candidate experience and is often intentionally deceptive. Stop substituting equitably compensated jobs with grandiosely titled demotions. Deception seen through the candidate lens can lead to an external view of your company as intentionally deceptive, and that perspective carries through.

And one quick word on the idea of ensuring that you also see your candidates as potential customers, as there are many times when they literally become potential critical customers, especially when your business is in business to business sales of products and services. Let me give you an example of my own experience here if I may. I have had situations where my candidate experience was absolute trash, and I remembered each one, thinking that there is no way this company can keep employees or get the best talent if this is the experience it is creating. I often consult with companies externally or advise on vendor guidelines and RFPs on experience management and HR software both internally and externally, depending on my role. And on several occasions, a company comes up that I had researched during my candidate experience with it, and I nix it as an option. And it's not a bitterness thing or a revenge thing—it's me being in a position to form a more well-informed opinion and then a more accurate recommendation. These are contracts potentially ranging from $20,000 to upwards of $1 million annually. But I remember the candidate experience, and I do my research, and I investigate the employee experience of these companies. I then make a recommendation based not only on the quality of the tool but also on the EVP of the company. As part of that recommendation, I also make a calculation of risk based on the potential turnover of customer experience support staff and key knowledge workers. In these cases, I am a potential customer or advising a potential customer. In short, there are many other people in my position out there, and it's not worth it to your organization's bottom line to refuse investing in making your employee experience and, embedded with it, your candidate experience better.

Remember, an experience with you begins the moment somebody simply meets you. For a candidate, that's the moment they complete your application and transmit it to your organization. You have the responsibility and the ability to design an experience for your candidates that you also want to carry through when they become employees. The ideal candidate situation is when somebody gets rejected and says, "I got rejected, but I had a really good experience with that company, and I would apply again."

A WORD ON INTERNAL CANDIDATES

It goes without saying that internal candidates often don't feel that they're being treated as well as external candidates when competing for the same roles. This can be a problem because organizations usually have amazing internal talent to move up through the ranks. Make sure that the experience for your internal candidates is comparable to the experience for external candidates. You don't want internal candidates to feel like the only way to move up or negotiate the level of compensation and benefits they desire is to come from the outside or by leaving and returning. Internal candidates need to feel that they have options to grow professionally within your organization, whether it be through an internal talent marketplace, development programs, or prioritized opportunities. They need to feel that they, too, have a voice and are seen equally for everything, including salary and benefit negotiations, if and when they join the candidate pool for a posted role. Their statuses as employees and candidates should be viewed separately and not be conflated in any way. Furthermore, a well-designed employee-experience strategy should not make them notice distinct differences in how they experience work as an employee and how they experience being an internal candidate. So, to emphasize this point clearly, when you think about how you design your candidate experience, please ensure that you design the process to be considerate about how you include and treat your internal candidates, too.

CHAPTER 9

I THINK I LOVE
TALENT PLANNING

Admittedly, employee talent is a broad topic, and we usually hear it discussed in the general context of managing, recruiting, and retaining the "best" employees. But I wouldn't be me if I didn't switch it up a bit, so let's talk about talent planning. It is not only one of the most important aspects of the employee experience but also one of the most lazily handled (yes, I said it!). Many companies have a succession crisis right now because they are reluctant to truly invest in vetting the line of leadership, in most cases, past the most senior executive levels. They operate under the assumption that changing the C-suite executives is the solution, but in reality, there are probably about five layers of problematic employees and managers who are impeding growth, innovation, and change at organizations. Of course, no company wants to remove all of its leaders—though, I can think of a few organizations in recent history where that might have been the actual solution.

The other problem with succession planning is the overwhelming prevalence of bias. Before you get defensive, hear me out for a minute. Talent and succession planning often come with a lot of unspoken and spoken sentiments, like, "This person reminds me of me," "He acts just like me," "This is/was my mentee," or "The idea of this person as a leader just makes me comfortable." Sound familiar? Yup. I hate to tell you, but these lines of thinking are chock-full of bias and, well, can lead to all kinds of nonsense.

Talent planning typically starts with performance management. And I'm just going to say it: most performance management processes right now are fundamentally broken. Most performance management systems I encounter these days I fondly refer to as Organizational Hunger Games, where bad behavior is rewarded unintentionally instead of good performance. Because companies make performance metrics so critical at the end of the year, the first issue they have baked in is a recency effect, where people do their best work at the end of the year when performance reviews are near. So they may be rewarded for a great fourth quarter even though their work was subpar at best throughout the rest of the year. It can also work in reverse, where the employee who has been performing highly all year has a difficult fourth quarter and then they are overlooked for rewards and increases simply based on their fourth-quarter performance.

Frankly, many performance review systems are too "gotcha!" I also genuinely believe that too many managers perversely enjoy the sneak attack. They prefer to "manage people out" based on one quarter or even one event of poor performance instead of providing continuous feedback to promote improvement throughout the year. This is what, at one point, was called "quiet firing," but really it was people managers too scared to do their jobs and have difficult conversations. I worked at one company where no form of performance plan was given to employees with a low rating. It created a situation in which an employee could be at the mercy of a bad manager who just did not like them, as there was no accountability metric for the manager.

The system assumed that all managers are good and well-intentioned people managers—but we know better, right? Right? That's a massive assumption. Of course, and this probably goes without saying, this kind of system tends to adversely affect underrepresented groups and groups that are considered more marginalized, as current workplace statistics show that they are less likely to hold the people manager roles and even less likely to hold more senior roles.

Continuous feedback is more important than annual performance reviews. Period. A system that does not create and build in accountabilities for continuous feedback is a broken performance management system. Imagine if a doctor worked by using the simple annual feedback model. The doctor sees something troubling in your tests but decides to wait for your next annual checkup to tell you about it. Ethics, anyone? Can you say lawsuit? Who could blame you? The bottom line is that organizations need to stop waiting for low performers to get worse (or magically get better on a wish and a prayer) while conversely hoping the good higher performers continue performing well just because they can. This is an insidious and short-sighted approach to performance management—and an easy way to actually lose your best talent. It's fine to let people know they need to improve, and if they demonstrate that, even with guidance, they still cannot improve, *then* it's much more humane and justifiable to let them go or reassign them. What's not fine is asking someone to do something and not providing the resources to do it, then punishing them for what they were not able to do. One of those resources? Feedback.

HIGH PERFORMERS VERSUS HIGH POTENTIALS

If you work at any organization, you probably have heard the terms *high-performing talent* or *high-potential talent*. You may wonder what these mysterious labels mean or how the powers that be are making these classifications. Well, let's dive into the difference between the two, how you assess them, and what it really means to be high potential or high performing. Let's begin by looking at them one by one.

High-performing talent is backward looking. This is key. High performance is based on assessing how an employee has performed over an established period to decide whether they have met or exceeded expectations or established goals for their particular role. The best way to assess this is based on available success metrics data, peer and/or client feedback, and, in ideal situations, notations of feedback conversations and check-ins over a given period. A high-performing-talent system recognizes outstanding performance and rewards it, as applicable, based on the role and the organizational culture. This system examines if the employee has had an impact on their role, on projects, on organizational growth and transformation, or on anything that is a critical element or key indicator of business success or progress. High-performing talent is generally celebrated with perks like bonuses, promotions, key job rotations, and more access to things that normally are not widely available to all employees, such as meetings or mentorship with executive leaders and key decision-makers. Good high-performing-talent data tends to be more objective to identify and measure, which makes it more likely to be evidence based. (Note: This data might *not* be objective if related performance and training support systems and processes are inherently biased and broken).

High-potential talent is forward looking. And it is much more of a . . . how shall I say it? . . . doozy, maybe? It aims to deduce whether an employee will positively impact their role and the organization in the future. The organization has identified preset knowledge, skills, abilities, and other competencies that it characterizes as helpful for the role going forward. If an employee appears to have all the right skills forecasted as high impact or as critical leadership capabilities, then the organization will determine that they have high potential.

Recognizing high-potential talent is much more difficult than recognizing high-performance talent because you are dealing with abstract beliefs and instincts instead of data that actually exists. It can be a bit chaotic because you don't necessarily have a lot of data (or anything of much substance) to go off of in making the high-potential determination. In fact, you might not have any past data at all, so you are essentially making an assumption, which, in most cases, is highly subjective and, yes . . . you guessed it . . . likely also highly problematic.

Can we be frank for a minute here? I'm so tired of hearing leaders talk about these "gut decisions." Your gut is not intended for decision-making. Your gut harbors a complex community of over a hundred trillion microbial cells, which influence human physiology, metabolism, nutrition, and immune function. You know what it is not set up for? Critical decisions about people. Isn't every single person you hire supposed to have high potential? Otherwise, why are you hiring them? For fun?

There's a world of biases that can be baked into the high-potential-talent designation, with key decision-makers implicitly asking themselves questions like, "Who looks like me? Who acts like me? Who reminds me of me?" Do leaders always tend to be introspective and ask themselves if they are, in fact, the person who can truly take the company in the intended direction? In my experience, the answer is no, so we get more of the same formula even when the times have changed. In fact, the transition years between 2019 and 2024 have been a clear demonstration of this, where the workforce has rapidly changed in needs and mindset, technology has shifted dramatically, and the way employees began working has shifted, but many key leaders demand that work remains the same, creating a massive incongruence between leaders and their workforces, muddling definitions of things like high potential, and creating problematic succession and talent planning.

The high-potential-talent designation quickly can become the enemy of DEI in all its forms. In general, people who are identified as high potential do not reflect underrepresented or institutionally marginalized groups. There are not enough representative people in leadership to mentor them, sponsor them, advocate for them, or see themselves in them. As a result, a lot of underrepresented people do not see themselves as potential leaders within their organizations. So it is imperative to be aware of the true reasons behind deeming somebody as having high potential.

Let's also not forget that potential does not mean success. If you buy a brand-new car to drive across the country, you do so knowing that it has the potential to get you to your destination. But that potential means nothing if you do not put gas in the car so that it can drive. You never went on the trip. Potential without evidence of action means absolutely nothing. It's a nice car, though!

A high-performing employee does not necessarily have high potential. I know I am throwing in some grenades here, so bear with me, but I'll repeat it again. Just because they're a high performer does not mean they'll be identified as having high potential. It could be that they're only transactional, they can do the job that is put in front of them, and they can do it well. But they might not necessarily have what it takes to go beyond that. They're just good at their current job. And let me be clear: that is not necessarily a bad thing if that is where their ambition lies and/or what their lifestyle prefers, or if they feel that they have met their own professional goal. High-potential designations are organizational, not personal, attributions.

Shall I throw another wrench into this equation? How about this one: your highest-potential people are not necessarily your best-performing people. A lot of high-potential individuals are identified early in their professional journeys, even before there is enough evidence to accurately predict future success. Think about the amazing athletes coming out of college in any given year. They go to the professional sports leagues as first- or second-round draft picks and are given lucrative contracts based on their potential, and everybody expects them to just ball out. But instead, they fizzle and end up eventually being traded or cut. Then, there are the athletes who get drafted in the lower rounds—or never drafted at all—but end up as athletic and hall-of-fame-level standouts. They were not necessarily seen as high potentials in college, but they were seen as good performers who would be given an opportunity to demonstrate performance (think accumulate league-level data) at lower salary levels and with riskier contracts, and it panned out well.

Now, when the high potential also turns out to be a top performer and one of the best ballers in the league, that's the ideal space that any athletic organization wants to be in. And that is the space that generally any organization wants to be in, no matter the industry or size. When your designated high-potential employee shows evidence of a high performance, they become high impact and at risk of regrettable loss (especially due to high recruiting demand), then you invest in them generously and strategically and put them into talent plans and succession lines. Where potential meets performance is your talent sweet spot.

IDENTIFYING TALENT AND FUTURE LEADERS

The old ways of talent and succession planning simply do not make sense. We have all this data, but organizations continuously ignore it to perpetuate the noise and nonsense. Effective planning requires accountability, which a lot of leaders and organizational decision-makers do not want (whether they want to admit it or not). In reality, there are a lot of people who are identified as having high potential too early, and they are flaming out, yet they are allowed to remain on a career path because leaders simply do not want to be wrong. Now the succession line is broken, and they are wondering why.

Your high-performing employees probably make up only about 25 percent of your talent pool. To identify them, here are some questions to prioritize in your conversations and discussions:

- Is this employee critical to business success?
- Is this employee consistent with good performance over time?
- Is this person seen as a leader within the team regardless of whether they have the title or not?
- Has the employee contributed significantly to key business initiatives that were critical to team success?
- Has the employee been able to save the company time and/or money?
- Has the employee been identified as a top performer within their team, within that division, or within that organization?
- If this person decided to leave the organization, would their loss be considered regrettable (as in, would we be sorry we lost that person)?
- Would that loss be considered preventable? For example, were there things that the organization could have done to make that person stay, like improving conditions; renegotiating; increasing salary, benefits, or bonuses; etc.?

High-potential talent is a relatively smaller group, likely only representing about 5 percent of your talent pool. So you must remember that it is a future-oriented group and a future-oriented concept that requires a lot of subjectivity. Ask yourself the following types of questions:

- Will this employee be critical in moving the team forward?
- Can the team member lead key initiatives that are critical to the team and the organization?
- Can this person with this skill set progress through the organization successfully?
- Is this person ready to move into the next line of succession outside of their current role?
- Can this person be successful in a role that has more responsibility and more leadership or management?
- Can this person lead through transformation and change?
- If this person left, would their leaving be seen as regrettable or preventable?

So where is the sweet spot for these classifications? Think about high performance and high potential as a Venn diagram. Your best talent typically lies in that little area where the circles overlap, which is likely only about 1 percent of your workforce. We are currently in this environment where "everybody is great and has high potential," but that just isn't accurate. Remember, the high-potential employee is not necessarily the high performer. To be brutally honest, if all your high potentials leave, that's fine. The highest levels of regrettable loss tend to be with the people who have a proven past of high performance and a proven future of high potential.

HIGH PERFORMANCE, HIGH POTENTIAL, AND THE EMPLOYEE EXPERIENCE

How does all this coincide with the employee experience? High-potential and high-performing talent identifications are important aspects of career growth, which are key performance indicators related to the employee experience. Organizations need to ensure that their people feel comfortable, are able to grow, and empowered to develop their careers. Employees want to know that their talents are being recognized and used effectively and efficiently by the organization. They want to be made aware of any changes that need to be made and receive feedback to make the necessary changes to help them be key contributors and their best selves at work.

Organizations must have structures in place to ensure that talent planning and performance identification are being done well and with process transparency. Unlike the recognition of high-performing talent, when it comes to recognizing high-potential talent, there are some challenges, in addition to the obvious biases, that leaders must think through. They need to consider whether to tell somebody when they have been identified as having high potential. What would happen if that person doesn't perform well in the future? Would they lose the high-potential designation? Are they taken off the list for promotion?

My recommendation is to not tell somebody that they're high potential. This recommendation aligns with most of the people that I've consulted and collaborated with on thought projects and research within this space. Remember, high potential is an organizational designation, not a personal one. It can create a pretty challenging, and sometimes ethical, conundrum. For instance, telling someone that they have high potential, and then investing resources in them, can create a self-fulfilling prophecy. You made an investment that bolstered their potential. On the other hand, what if you make the investment and they turn out to be a dud? Do you then declassify them as not having high potential? In addition, is there an expiration date for high potential? Should we place some type of temporary boundary around high potential, such as the current quarter or a specific position? These are just some of the many questions that drive my skepticism of high-potential talent.

We are setting up a lot of people for failure, which is the antithesis of any good employee-experience strategy. As I have said before, some people simply don't make the cut when it comes time to prove themselves through performance via success metrics. They might have had high potential, but like a car with no gas, they're just not going anywhere. Now they are taking a spot in this designated program that probably should have been given to someone better equipped for future growth and high organizational impact. For example, think about a data analyst who provides all of the background information but never gives the presentations. The person giving the presentations is identified as having high potential, while the data analyst is not. But the presenter could not do their job without that data analyst. The impact is the function of two people and not one, yet you have only identified the one because you have not properly defined what high potential is. Maybe one should be identified as having high potential in leadership and the other as having high potential related to building the data system across the company. This would be an innovative way of talent planning, but most companies are stuck in an antiquated, biased, and industrial revolution–era model of what employee potential and performance look like.

These are discussions that organizations need to have and decisions they need to make. They need to take a stance on this topic. It's not easy, and it's still a fairly new part of the talent planning and employee experience discussions. There's a lot of research being done in the user experience, employee experience, and HR spaces about this topic, so I am hopeful about the prospect of this becoming more of a continuous and evolving conversation, and hopefully we'll get more answers over time.

One last piece of advice: if your organization has a structure in place for identifying both high-potential and high-performing talent, make sure that you also have a next step. What is the next step for your high performers? Is it a promotion? A reward? A bonus? You need to have something in place or else it's completely useless. You want to make sure that it's done in a way in which there is a direction and a path—and you need an end goal to that path. Also, the reward for good work should not just be more work.

As for high-potential talent, if you are going to take the time to identify these people and justify the classification, then you must have some sort of program to move them into and through. In other words, take that empty gas tank to the gas station and fill it up! This could look like training programs or development programs. You might even try rotation programs, where multiple development programs are created for those who are considered both high-potential and high-performing talent, which can also help you assess more specific skills and role fits to set these employees up for success. Mixing both high performers and high-potential employees into these programs can also help them learn from one another, maximizing the ability to have more successful overall talent outcomes.

There's a lot to think about and critical decisions to be made continuously about talent, but it's extremely important because lack of career growth and failing to be recognized for their talent and contributions are some of the top reasons employees leave organizations. Failing to think about talent planning and how it falls into the employee experience leaves a major gap for retaining amazing talent. Not to mention that when succession lines aren't planned well or invested in at multiple levels in the organization (even those that consider themselves as "flat"), you end up with a succession crisis . . . and I'm not talking about the TV show. Succession crises are detrimental to organizational success and culture, and they can indeed destroy a company's customer and employee brand perception. In short, it's not worth the shortcuts.

Good talent is everything.

CHAPTER 10

I THINK I LOVE RECOGNITION

G iving recognition and feedback are two of the easiest and most cost-effective investments a company can make to bolster the employee experience, but many organizations have no processes in place to make it happen. Yes, you may have tenure or milestone acknowledgements, but meaningful recognition is about making people feel consistently seen, listened to, and valued—not insulting them with useless pizza and ice cream socials. In addition, recognition should not just be aligned with the organization, as in the case of milestone and tenure awards. Workplace recognition should be person centered, with a focus on behaviors and actions that create wins at many levels. Recognition is one of the highest forms of feedback.

I often find that employees have no idea whether they are doing well in their positions because they have not received any feedback. But it should be just as easy to tell somebody that they did a good job as it is to tell them that their performance really sucks—though, somehow, we tend to lean toward the latter. Even if it does not feel like a natural process, recognition can become part of your organization's culture, as a standard aspect of leadership and management. Unfortunately, it is sorely lacking in the current business culture. Feeling valued has a legitimate, long-term impact for both employees and organizations, and it shows up in organizational metrics and people analytics through success indicators, like positive retention rates and high engagement scores. This is also why recognition is a significant aspect of the employee experience and a crucial part of any employee-experience strategy.

CRAFTING A RECOGNITION PROGRAM

Putting an effective recognition system in place requires an investment of time and resources. For some organizations, that starts with tearing down the existing performance management system that feeds into the problems. Broken systems can create workplace trauma by putting good employees through bad experiences. There is nothing worse than seeing people being celebrated for their mistreatment of others. Think about the employee who responds rudely to a coworker who shares a suggestion with them, or the employee is rewarded later for the idea that they actually stole from a coworker. Employees remember these bad experiences.

Children are pros at asking for recognition. When my daughter (a first-grader at the time of this writing) wants me to recognize her latest dance, she runs up to me and asks me to watch her . . . nonstop . . . then demands my feedback on the spot. Yet as we get older, we grow less comfortable with seeking out acknowledgment. We even become more comfortable with receiving criticisms than accepting compliments and celebrating wins. That child in all of us never goes away, though. We all want to be recognized for a job well done, and organizations need a system that leans into that, recognizes their employees' humanness, and puts good and transparent processes in place to ensure it happens. Recognition is a key win for everyone involved.

A lot of organizational leaders think that rewarding employees requires only financial incentives, but that is the reason we are in this dilemma. Financial incentives, such as bonuses and spot awards, are great forms of recognition, but employees are also highly motivated by nonmonetary forms of recognition, such as statements and announcements of gratitude for specific wins, peer callouts, social recognition, and acknowledgement— even recognition through technology, with technical-access badges and profile designations. They want feedback. They want that dopamine rush that comes from feeling appreciated and recognized for their input and the effort made toward the accomplishment of a goal.

The bottom line of recognition is that people want to *be seen and feel valued*. Financial incentives are good, but they generally can be held for the most impactful forms of performance and can serve as a diamond standard for employees to aspire to achieve. This allows for the reservation of these investments to optimize performance while not ignoring the several small, everyday wins that employees get to contribute to the bigger, overall picture—all in pursuit of organizational success. It also allows the organization to motivate the performance it is desiring rather than unintentionally rewarding bad behavior and shortcuts through short-term financial gains. This creates a more balanced and democratized culture of recognition, which is a key contributor to excellent employee experiences.

REWARDING THE BARE MINIMUM

Even good recognition systems have potential issues to look out for, especially if monetary rewards are involved. For instance, when giving out bonuses for meeting goals, organizations need to be careful about recognizing people for the right things. If you've noticed a pattern where one person is consistently meeting milestones while everyone else struggles, you need to seek clarity about the reasons behind the anomaly. If you keep recognizing one person for meeting the same goal over and over again, with no understanding of how or why they are doing it, yet ignore the fact that nobody else is able to perform at the same level, you run the risk of encouraging the wrong behavior. Instead of rewarding the behavior that you are trying to recognize, which would be the accomplishment of set goals, you may actually be rewarding the bad behavior that it takes to get there. It's important to recognize when something seems wrong or off. If you have a team of five and one person is repeatedly hitting it out of the ballpark, even out of the country, that warrants some further investigation instead of blind recognition. You could have four people who are working their behinds off within the system and doing all the right things. Yet you're rewarding the behavior of the person who's taking shortcuts.

A high level of discernment is vital when crafting an employee recognition program because organizations can easily fall into a cycle of recognizing people for doing the bare minimum. This is an especially big problem in sales and talent acquisition spaces, where organizations often set relatively unreasonable targets and focus on them without consideration for the behavior it takes to reach them. Even if unethical behaviors are used to reach targets, they are still rewarded because the end metric overrides the process.

These actions take away from the people who are willing to go the extra mile the right way. Instead, organizations get these short-term gains, but at what long-term cost?

MANAGERS AND RECOGNITION

The right answer for managers to be better at recognition is a continuous feedback system that recognizes employees at various times of the year. Think about walking to work in a big city. As you move through the streets, you are one of many—until someone speaks to you specifically and asks how you are feeling. Then, you no longer feel like one of many. Instead, you feel seen as an individual. Performance reviews should not be a surprise—whether good or bad. Feedback systems cannot consist of "gotcha" moments that result in unexpected promotions or layoffs. It should not be a game.

To combat implicit recency effects in current performance review and annual merit systems, managers need to recognize (or correct) employees as soon as possible after the performance occurs. Managers should be making consistent notes regarding feedback and recognition as a part of their role in the company. That way, when it comes to doing annual reviews, they are not tasking a busy employee with the burden of trying to remember every single thing that they did over the course of a year.

Even if it's just a quick comment from a manager who says, "You know, you did a really great job on that project," the difference between the experience of this recognition versus a manager who says nothing at all is like night and day. You want managers who empower, enrich, and value the employees they are responsible for. Employees want managers who treat them like they matter.

ONE SIZE DOES NOT FIT ALL

It is not hard to give meaningful recognition, but it's important to give your chosen methods some consideration. For instance, sending a short thank-you card can be a great option, but it still needs to be meaningful—which means, don't just send everybody a general recognition card. At some point, it loses its meaning, so there is no true value when recognition is warranted. Another method I see a lot is public recognition in front of the entire team or office. But this can have serious anti-diversity implications. Yes, some people love all the bells and whistles. They want to hear their names called publicly and hear the applause of their colleagues. But this type of attention might make other people uncomfortable.

Case in point, there are cultural differences in how people like to be recognized. For some people, being called out in front of others makes them feel ashamed and embarrassed. I understand these feelings very well. Culturally, recognition is something I personally still struggle with. Many people of color, for example, are taught to keep their heads down and just do their work. They are discouraged from seeking or even welcoming recognition. In fact, groups that tend to face more institutional marginalization tend to be taught to not seek out recognition, as it may be detrimental to their professional invisibility. They tend to be taught to create value in the quietest way possible so as to not call attention to themselves. And this message is often internalized and then reinforced by organizations that refuse to recognize their employees but then force them to write annual self-evaluations.

Now, a manager may be responsible for an employee who culturally does not want to be the center of attention and another employee who loves to be called out. They both work hard and perform well, so the manager wants to recognize them. If you choose to recognize them both publicly over the objections of one, you may appear to show favoritism to the one who enjoys attention. Instead, find a happy middle ground. It may just be calling out the names, but not going deeply into details at the time, and then sending a group email with more detailed information later. My biggest recommendation is also to have one-on-one meetings with both employees prior to any potential public callout.

I know it can sometimes feel harder than you would like to tailor recognition, but you should make a real effort to do it well. Recognition needs to be in your leadership DNA. Get to know your people as well, so you can identify the nuances of individual and collective motivation. This investment does not have to be huge. Again, people just want to feel seen—even if just for a moment. This is, for example, why social media is so addictive to many people.

A WORD ON THE MISUSE AND
ABUSE OF RECOGNITION

When it comes to leaders, recognition and what they are rewarded for can become crucial elements that ultimately drive organizational culture. Leaders often do not pivot because they see their own behavior—however good or bad—being rewarded. So they continuously do what has been previously recognized, even if it means mistreating their own employees. Leaders are in the unfair position of not being told the truth about their actions from their subordinates or even other leaders; though, unfortunately, in many cases the yes-men are monsters of their own creation. Even public actions outside of the workplace may go unchecked because work has become such a big part of our social identity. This is how company culture gets broken from the top. When bad behaviors are reinforced, they become part of the organizational fabric, which creates problems both inside and outside of the organization. All because of toxic recognition.

A lack, or misuse, of recognition, is often tied to toxic work environments. It is almost like a virus takes over your people, where they begin to realize that the only road to recognition and getting ahead is to emulate the negative things that others are doing. Now, whatever that toxic trait is, everybody has inherited it. It has mutated from a virus to a part of your organizational DNA. You start attracting toxic people to the company, further perpetuating the problem. Your organization is now so sick that it's terminal and unable to heal because it would take five layers of leaders to be replaced before there is even a chance of getting better.

Look at the tech industry in the 2000s. Companies had been rewarding growth for more than a decade, measuring the head count as an indicator of success. But it was an unsustainable way to grow. They were growing their head counts at an alarming rate, but they were being celebrated, recognized, and rewarded for it—so they did not stop. Until they had no choice. It was an unsustainable amount of growth and the industry had to rebalance—it was inevitable. The result? Massive layoffs across the industry. Their own talent paid the price. Along with the loss of talent went the façade of the tech industry's progressive culture and top-tier employee-experience reputation.

These problems can also extend to consulting companies that advise organizations. They impact the employee experience with their data, but they twist it to match the story you want to tell, instead of letting the data speak for itself and tell its own story. Companies continually were rewarding these organizations for the skewed data that didn't tell the whole truth—data that, as it turned out, poisoned already culturally and strategically sick organizations. And it cost them millions in consulting fees to get sicker. The result? Massive cutbacks and layoffs across industries. Again, the average employee paid the price for bad leadership decisions.

RECOGNITION AND THE EMPLOYEE EXPERIENCE

Recognition is a big part of the employee experience. Employees who feel appreciated also recognize their value to the organization. Recognized employees are often willing to step up and use as many tools as they have in their tool belt because they have an understanding of and a greater appreciation for—if you will—their relationship and value to the company and even potentially the company's overall strategy. Non-monetary recognition is an unlimited resource, but many companies choose to ignore their people instead. It's as easy as a kind word or email. Recognize what's happening within the workplace. Recognize changes that are occurring and the people who are still there despite how hard it can be to work through organizational transformation. Simply giving people a genuine word of gratitude is often enough to sustain an employee and help them have a positive employee experience. Sometimes it's just the little things.

It's not hard to see how the abuse or misuse of recognition and how behavior is rewarded, especially at the leadership and C-suite levels, can severely impact the employee experience. Like everything covered so far in this book, which also will be discussed later, the key takeaway is that nothing related to the employee experience exists in a vacuum. Every decision that an organization makes is crucial to the evolution of its employee-experience strategy, and if you learn nothing else from this chapter, be set in the understanding that recognition is foundational to the employee experience such that failure to properly develop a culture of recognition makes it almost impossible to maintain organizational trust and sustain or execute a functional employee-experience strategy. Like any other key organizational operations investment, recognition is not hard to do well when done intentionally and strategically, but the impact of not doing it or doing it badly has far more dire consequences than most leaders realize.

CHAPTER 11

I THINK I LOVE WORK-LIFE BALANCE

The employee experience is about helping people be their most productive selves in the workplace, and work-life balance must be part of that experience. Though there is much debate about what work-life itself actually means (and whether it even exists), I am here to tell you that it is a real thing, but it looks very different for different people. When organizations provide flexible options, like remote work and customizable wellness options, they empower employees to craft their own work-life balance and be their best selves both inside and outside of work.

WORK-LIFE BALANCE

Work-life balance refers to the sense of time and impact between what you do as an employee and what you do when you are completely outside of your work role. The sense of balance itself is something that the employee maintains a level of control over, though the work side of the equation is still highly influenced by workload, stress, management, and professional responsibilities. I want to be clear in what I mean by work-life balance. We often try to explain it too rigidly as an even distribution of work and nonwork life, but that is not accurate. My definition is balancing your life at work with your roles and responsibilities outside of work. It's about having the ability to prioritize the elements of life that bring you joy, fulfillment, or self-care. Maybe you are a parent, and your kids are your fulfillment, or you are a pet parent who gets joy from your cats. Maybe your self-care looks like a buzzing social life with your friends or just lying in your bed and taking the longest, most satisfying naps ever. Whatever your definition of "outside of work" is and whatever your sense of joy and self-care look like, balance is about honoring those things and giving yourself the time and space to indulge in and enjoy them in a way that is completely disconnected from your day-to-day role as an employee.

Whatever you create in your life that brings you balance is fine, and how that balance happens is different and subjective for everyone. For some people, elements of work even bring them satisfaction and joy. They get into a state of flow with their work responsibilities and may spend more time at the office than other people do. Some people may see their evenings and weekends as overwork, but that's not how it feels to them. They find their balance in the time that they have outside of work to sleep in, or hang out, or play with their kids or pets, which is perfectly fine. See, we do not get to dictate work-life balance to other people. It is customized to what we each deem to be important, and it can look different at different life stages. It can look different at twenty-one years old than it does at forty years old. It can look different before you have children than it does after you become a parent. It may even look different depending on the day, the month, or the year. As our lives evolve, we constantly seek to rebalance and reimagine our boundaries. Then, we must clearly communicate what those boundaries are. Your balance gets off when boundaries are pushed without permission or agency and when the joyful things begin to feel burdensome. A key to understanding where your balance and your sense of equilibrium lies is tapping into how you feel in the transition between work and nonwork activities over a sustained period. For example, if you get to a point in which you feel a sense of dread, heaviness, and, in some cases, physical pain at the prospect of returning to work, or if you have a sense of fear that you may not catch back up from taking a break, then you need to examine your work-life balance boundaries.

We can get lost in the word *balance* and the word *life*, but they tie into the element of self-care, which is extremely important. When we talk about workplace trauma and work-life balance, we must also talk about the idea of self-care. Self-care is rooted in the idea of healing the mind and body and allows people to pour into themselves in a selfishly unselfish way. You may be asking, "What does this have to do with employee experience?" Well, employees—from frontline to executive—cannot bring their best, most productive selves to work if they are functioning on empty. Functioning that way increases risks for mistakes, indecision, and counterproductive work behaviors, like presenteeism (lost productivity resulting from employees not fully functioning in the workplace due to illness, injury, or some other condition); absenteeism; disagreeableness; aggression, sabotage; and even violence. Work takes energy, and that is the energy of the whole person—mind, body, spirit, and soul. Well-being is an operational imperative tied directly to any organization's bottom line.

SELF-CARE AND CREATING WELLNESS PROGRAMS

Organizations need to create the space and time for employees to be able to refill their proverbial cups so that they can both pour into others (especially in the case of people managers) and pour into their own work. What does self-care look like, then? It may look like travel or spending time with family. For some people, working out is the answer, but for others, it's just having time away from work. A critical thing I need to reiterate here is that companies should not take a one-size-fits-all approach self-care and well-being. You cannot happy hour or yoga your employees to death and call it a wellness program. This is why organizational wellness programs must become more inclusive. Sometimes wellness is as simple as what a person has to do to give their brain a rest. Organizations have the power to give employees options.

My biggest advice for creating a wellness program is ensuring that it pours back into employees what their work takes from them. Think of it as recharging a phone. Wellness is how your employees charge themselves back up so they can work faster, think more clearly, be more critical, and optimize their performance. If you are working from a place of building good employee experiences that are people centered, then you will create employee wellness programs that empower people to feel like they can be their most productive selves at work.

Another element of work-life balance that often gets ignored is financial wellness, as the inability to pay bills can have far-reaching effects on employee well-being. For example, recent research by Workhuman and BLK Men in Tech found that many underrepresented and historically marginalized groups within the tech industry typically take care of more than their immediate nuclear families. As members of communities that tend to be more communal and collectivistic, they are often financially responsible for other members of their extended families. Organizations typically only think about their employees taking care of nuclear families, but these employees may be dealing with far more in reality. Financial advice and related wellness programs need to be tailored to the actual needs of employees, meeting them where they are, not where one may expect them to be.

A good employee experience is never loud. The employee experience always gets quieter when people feel that they are being poured into because they feel ready to work. Work is such a big part of people's identities, and it should not have to take away from their overall quality of life. We can do better.

REMOTE WORK CAN WORK

Remote work can play a big role in providing employees with the flexibility they need to carve out their own brand of work-life balance, yet we constantly see pushback against it, as if it is a new and foreign concept. Even though most people were introduced to remote work during the pandemic, many employees had been working remotely for several years prior. Let me also point out that working remotely does not mean working away from the office 100 percent of the time. It just means working from different locations, which is nothing new. There have been times when I sat in my physical office talking to people who are in different countries and completely different time zones. In essence, I was working remotely regardless of the fact that I was sitting in an office. I was on a video call having these work conversations. The main differences for me between working from the office and working remotely everyday was that I had to get up, get dressed, and commute to the office. And those differences for me just meant lost time and aggravation from traffic. So the argument that remote work cannot work is absolute foolishness. Now, obviously, not every job can be done remotely. It is also not the best option for everyone because some people don't thrive in a remote environment. But remote work has been a welcome reality for many of people for a long time.

Workplace flexibility is the way of the future, so organizations just need to recognize that remote work is a natural progression of having more technology and doing more business across the world. I get it—many organizations didn't account for this and made a lot of real-estate investments, and yes, I'm sure seeing your organization's name on a high-rise in a big city is enthralling. But look, work evolves, and, unfortunately, sometimes it takes a whole pandemic to kick all of us, organizations and employees, forward—even when those who hold the power may not be at their highest state of preparedness. The manufacturing model of standing over folks and monitoring their every move just no longer works. The marginal lift you might get in productivity is not sustainable and does nothing to engender trust or growth in employees. Plus, that whole management model is more about the manager than it is about the employee. And the more you do it, the more you tighten your grip around a person and the more you push them toward leaving the company. The reality is that, even if not done 100 percent of the time, remote work (or some iteration of it that promotes flexibility) is the future.

Everybody likes talking about this so-called war for talent, and remote work, or at least location flexibility, must be part of winning that "war." It's an overt way of investing in and committing to the employee experience. I recall an incident in which a peer was not feeling well and requested to work the rest of the day from home. Even though he had worked from home many times before, and even after work hours, the supervisor refused his request. Furthermore, this was the same supervisor who was constantly asking him to power up his computer from home at night to work on one task or another. I saw his commitment to this role and his desire to leave change almost overnight. It was not long until he decided to leave the job. It is ridiculous for leaders to not trust their employees to do their jobs. If you're hiring a bunch of people that you can't trust unless they are right in front of you, that's a problem. And if you don't trust anybody you work with, you might be the problem. And if that last sentence hurts, you are definitely the problem.

This perspective of "if I can't see you, you aren't working" is archaic. And I have news for you. In open offices everywhere right now, workers are sitting at their computers with headphones on watching Netflix or listening to music. Yes, they are getting their work done, but they also recognize that they are being paid to just sit in the office and stare at a screen even when there are lulls at work or they are waiting on something to be able to move their project forward. This is what happens when location becomes more important than the person. And when location and a manager's ability to see an employee become more important than the person or the quality of the work that they produce, then the issue is not and has never been performance productivity or innovation; it is simply about control.

Here is the truth: people actually can be working more efficiently from home, freeing up room on the highways for people who cannot work remotely. There are people who get power from overseeing others doing their work. The focus on quality outcomes is too often lost to insecurity. And what's worse is that this insecurity and need for control overwrite the available research and data that support remote work and flexible location policies as key drivers of better overall business outcomes.

Trust allows for autonomy, and when people feel trusted by their leaders and believe that their organizations have their best interests at heart, they will keep working productively. Most people don't naturally want to slack off. They will do what is expected of them when they feel trusted to do it. Now, there's nothing wrong with a periodic check-in and having more communication, but if you don't trust your employees, then you are essentially just running an expensive adult day care.

When trying to reason with leaders about remote work, I often hear them champion watercooler conversations in the workplace.

They characterize these communications as creative, where ideas and innovations are born. Lies. All convenient lies. Why do I say that? Because these are the same conversations that leaders called time wasters only a few short years ago. In fact, some of them put policies in place to prevent congregation at the watercooler. I have yet to be in a workplace where watercooler conversations led to any sort of significant work-related collaboration, but maybe that's just me. There's plenty of talk about the weekend, cake in the break room, kids, and whatever Coffee Judy is talking about that day. But there's little talk about work.

Let's get real. A lot of organizations build monuments of greatness to themselves, and those monuments are often buildings. They plaster their names across them, and the bigger the building, the bigger the name. In fact, they are not just building a building, they are building a campus—a legacy. A place for their employees to work and play. For leaders, I am sure there is nothing like walking into one of these monuments and being recognized by everyone inside. But then, they go upstairs to the forty-second floor in a private suite with five secretaries and have the nerve to say that they are having the exact same experience as the hundreds of people downstairs working in their cubicles. They say, "I work really well in the office, and you should, too." Well, of course they do. But leaders need to recognize that their experience is not the same.

Let me get a little more real for a moment, and don't worry, I have a brush to share in case there are any ruffled feathers. When a lot of leaders talk about remote work, what they are not saying is that remote work is a privilege that only extends (*and should only extend*) to them. Just tell the truth. It is your privilege. The rules are different for you. There are high-tech executives demanding that their employees return to work while they continue to work from an island in the Caribbean or the Pacific. None of this is missed on employees—especially the most talented ones and even the most devoted ones.

Organizations must dig into their policies and think about creating an environment that is flexible and allows for people to not necessarily be in the same room all the time but still be productive. The pandemic era showed us that even organizations that never offered remote work before did so when they had to. There are two things that really make remote work successful. One is training, and the other is an investment in technology. Managers need training on how to manage different people with different needs. Managers need to understand how to deal with teams that are distributed across various locations. Here is the good news: younger generations already have much more experience dealing with highly distributed social networks and are coming in with a much better skill set related to dealing with and managing this type of diverse, geographic distribution.

Most importantly, you cannot expect remote work to work with janky technology. Yup, I said janky. Get out of the dark ages because during the pandemic era, work-support technology advanced from what seems like 1930 to 2025 in the blink of an eye and is still going well ahead of what we can see in the present. Organizations must invest in technology that allows people to do remote work correctly. The technology is out there. And the truth is, many organizations have some of it already built into what they're doing. They just have to decide whether or not they want to make it a real investment.

FLEXIBILITY AND THE EMPLOYEE EXPERIENCE

Companies have spent more than a decade telling people that remote work was not a possibility. Yet they quickly made it work during the pandemic. As a result, employees realized that their organizations had been lying to them. Their reasonable accommodations could have been met all the while, yet their leaders chose not to meet them. Now these same leaders want their employees to forget their lies and go back into the office just because. Why? That's not a hypothetical question. Why do you *really* want your workers back in the physical office?

We have the talent and ability to do remote work and, in turn, help people craft their ideal work-life balance, which leads to a quieter and more fulfilling employee experience. That employee experience quiet comes from being set up for real success which allows you to be more engaged, productive, and focused. I implore and encourage organizations to stop fighting remote work or the creation of location flexibility. Flexibility sees everyone as a human. Return to office mandates sees everyone as a number. It takes into consideration the fact that everyone's work-life balance looks different. Work is not about a location. That is the model that companies have married themselves to for so long, but it is time for a change. Work is the effort tied to a set outcome or outcomes. Explore how greater flexibility can increase and diversify the people who come into your organization and improve how you can retain talent.

Your future of work, your employee experience, and your EVP depend on it.

CHAPTER 12

I THINK I LOVE DIVERSITY, EQUITY, AND INCLUSION (DEI)

Diversity, Equity, and Inclusion (DEI) (also referred to in some companies as Equity, Diversity, and Inclusion or Diversity, Equity, Inclusion, and Belonging has become a hot and controversial topic in the corporate world, especially in the mid- to post-pandemic period. Its controversial nature is somewhat exaggerated, as it is often given performance-level attention to score political points at the expense of those for whom the concepts, functions, and programs are designed to help. In terms of DEI as a corporate function, we are still far behind in how these issues are prioritized—often by design. The high rate of turnover that we have witnessed in the world of DEI professionals within designated corporate functions, generally within two to three years of being hired, no doubt results from the feelings of lack of tangible program support and the general inability to make a sustainable impact on organizational strategies. In many cases, no matter how seemingly well-intentioned these organizational endeavors into DEI are, their lack of impact (and, yes, success) can sometimes be due to circular logic and unfortunate self-fulfilling prophecies. As a result, many DEI-based programs and initiatives are coming across as more performative than genuine means for change and growth. A fragile plug in a raging dam if you will.

But how can this be different? Is DEI a lost cause? The answer is no, it absolutely does not have to be. Allow me to offer some thoughts and advice on why and how this relates to a successful employee-experience strategy. Let's start here: reframing how we think about DEI.

REFRAMING THE DEI QUESTION

Let's begin by reframing the typical foundational DEI question: how can we, or should we, be more diverse in how we recruit in our organization? Ah, here comes the defenses, right? Let's try this another way by asking this question: how can we find people to bring into our organization who can help us develop more creative and innovative approaches to reach our business-critical outcomes? Ask yourself that question. Now ask it again. Much more room for discussion and ideation, right? But here is the thing—they are the exact same questions. One version just has the words in it that trigger the political debates and heuristic biases, and the other feels more business related and outcome driven. The goal and intent behind both questions are the same, the process to solve both questions is the same, and the initiatives to get to an outcome related to both questions are the same—but in the latter question, the distraction that sparks performative action, grandstanding, and bias is removed. Looking at it that way, can you see how the debates around DEI are completely made up?

DEI is an outcome of making decisions related to your overall employee experience. It is the result of carefully thinking through and tying key decisions related to programs, policies, and processes to business outcomes within the context of people. If you want a more diverse customer base for a product, this is the exact strategic approach that you take, and the same goes for employees; though, for some reason, many organizational leaders cannot (or refuse to) make that connection. DEI is a product of a brilliant employee-experience strategy—it's not an operational input. It is through reframing this thinking can we make progress on changing the formulaic approach to selecting and retaining employees.

IT IS NOT YOUR SPACE

Though some aspects of DEI can be complicated, as a whole, the concept of maintaining a diverse and inclusive workplace is really quite simple. For instance, there is a lot of discussion about the lack of people from historically marginalized or underrepresented groups sitting on corporate boards. You have global companies boldly claiming an inability to craft a diverse board. I ask, are they not able or not willing? There are whole continents and areas of the world filled with Black and Brown people. There is an entire area of the world filled with Asian people. Between India and China alone, there are billions of people, yet you want me to believe that you cannot find one qualified non-White person to sit on your board? Please.

Let's look at another simple solution to another nonexistent problem . . . one of the most common impediments of DEI progress. Whenever companies begin having discussions about the need for more diverse people, an almost inevitable chorus of pushback erupts from the people who benefit from the current system.

This pushback stems from the belief that a diverse individual will come into the organization and take their space. But here is the simple part of that equation: the space never belonged to them in the first place. If I am hired to join a company, I come in and take *a* space within the organization, not *your* space. This is the type of rhetoric that makes underrepresented and historically marginalized groups feel compelled to apologize for their presence within the corporate environment. As an organizational leader, you have a responsibility to make this argument a moot point and advocate for better.

We must move people away from their irrational fear of the word *diversity*. It is the fear that change will somehow diminish individual standing, and this fear can thrive in any environment where there is a majority population, particularly a group that is more likely to directly or indirectly benefit from institutional structures that subjugate other smaller groups. The underrepresented or historically marginalized group will always be considered a threat. For example, I attended an HBCU (historically Black college and universities) as an international Trinidadian student, along with other international students of African descent or who were from the African diaspora from Jamaica, the Bahamas, and other countries. Collectively, we were an underrepresented group at our HBCU, and we were often seen as a threat by some. I had some African American students tell me directly that I was not Black. None of these people were racist, or at least didn't think that they were being racist or prejudiced, but they had this irrational fear that we were taking their places. I would jokingly respond that my ancestors were just dropped off one stop earlier than theirs, but I knew that their words stemmed from a survival instinct—the same instinct that tells us to run, fight, or freeze when we experience discomfort. When the majority of people in a workplace are experiencing discomfort, it can be hard for them to fathom that their fears are irrational. But if you allow those fears to impact your organization, you will miss out on the innovation and creativity that diversity in all of its forms brings.

Neurodiversity offers an excellent example of missed opportunities brought on by fear or discomfort. People who are autistic sometimes have the ability to see patterns much faster than other people. They can be amazing data scientists, but you won't hire them because you felt that they were "strange" in the interview. Your organization can lose incredible talent because your decision-makers lack the ability to cast aside their fears of someone who is different. They put too much weight on their own feelings, however irrational, instead of considering how that individual could work for and with them. My own son has autism, and though I still don't understand all that I would like to about his personal experiences, helping him has taught me a lot about managing people who are considered neurodiverse. The solutions that I use with him can also be used in the workplace to bridge communication gaps.

Fears and feelings have no place in DEI because they contribute in two harmful ways. First, you are telling one group something that they already know, and second, you are trying to make the other group feel comfortable. Humans need to get better with discomfort; it is what helps us innovate and thrive. When you put your hand on a hot stove, the discomfort tells you to remove it because it is dangerous, and then you go off and cook, using the heat from the stove without burning yourself. We have gotten so used to always being comfortable that it has warped our sense of ethics when it comes to diversity. The feelings have become performances, which does nothing but diminish the credibility of DEI. I hate the tragedy of a pandemic, but I am appreciative of the conversations that have occurred as a response to it. People are finally saying the quiet things out loud, especially those from underrepresented and historically marginalized groups. These are not new conversations for them, just conversations they have been taught not to have if they want to survive in general, including at work. They have been taught to manage their own discomfort to ensure that those around them have comfort. Unfortunately, there are still a lot of organizational leaders who resist those conversations, but they are necessary to reach the crucial business outcomes that stem from constructive conflict, innovation, and creativity.

BEAUTIFUL MUSIC

Most organizations prefer to focus on the diversity aspect of the DEI equation because it is the easiest to measure, track, and report on. Equity can be reported in similar ways, businesswise, to diversity if you choose to focus on the numbers through things like compensation and parity studies or audits. For the purposes of this discussion, I will discuss the diversity and inclusion elements of DEI more specifically and not the equity element for reasons previously discussed in terms of measurement and corporate conceptualizations. Inclusion is a more subjective concept and can be a beast unto itself. Here is the thing: you don't necessarily need diversity (or even equity) for commonly used inclusion measures and indicators to be high. Think about it—if you have a homogeneous group of people and you ask them if they feel included in the group, of course your inclusion scores are more likely to be high. Conversely, when there are high levels of diversity in environments left to their own devices, with no real organizational or cultural support, you are likely to have low inclusion scores in spite of the high levels of diversity. And I want to stress this part—the feature of organizational and cultural support is key with inclusion. High levels of inclusion will only coincide with high levels of diversity when an effort is made on the part of the organization to provide institutional support for understanding, tolerance, and learning, which then fosters safety, trust, and innovation. Inclusion is not a stand-alone measure of your diversity efforts. It may be a key indicator, but to measure inclusion requires a focus on context—looking at codependent variables, such as culture, psychological safety, ethics, leadership support, institutional investment, and leadership representation. Make no mistake—the most fulfilling part of DEI occurs when diversity and inclusion are both present.

There is a popular saying within the DEI space: "Diversity is being asked to the dance, and inclusion is being asked to dance." I think inclusion actually goes a few steps further. It is also the understanding that I can decline your invitation to the dance, and you will be okay with that. I can even go to the dance and choose to sit down the entire time instead of dancing with you, and you will also be okay with that. Inclusion is accepting people for who they really are and where they are, so they can bring their authentic selves into the workplace. With DEI, your organization is trying to ensure that diverse people, with diverse backgrounds and diverse ways of thinking, are all working toward the same goal. And I cannot stress this point enough: that point in your DEI journey is the sweet spot for amazing creativity, innovation, and productivity.

Real, tangible inclusion happens at the point where all the noise finally becomes beautiful music.

WATCH OUT FOR THE F-WORD

I cannot discuss DEI and not talk about the word *fit*. I am always wary when I hear the word *fit* come up in a workplace conversation. Is he a good fit for this role? Will she fit in with our team? You may not realize this, but in more cases than most care to admit, here is the translation of that term: you don't remind me of me, and you do not remind me of everything that feels familiar to me, so you will not fit.

We often tell ourselves that biases are simply unconscious, but this entire fit narrative is a conscious decision. No matter how *unconscious* your bias is, *your subsequent actions related to that bias are 100 percent conscious.* You decided that your comfort and your familiarity were more important than another person's skills, background, or ability to get an opportunity. You decided that being comfortable is more important to you than considering whether this person, all qualifications being equal, can really make an impact on your organization.

Being uncomfortable can be a good thing. Sometimes you need people to challenge your thinking and your worldview to be innovative, disruptive, and competitive. This is especially true in any organization and in times when we are seeing the rapid growth in various technologies across sectors, where the need for evolution and change is tantamount to survival. Inclusion in your organization is on you as a leader.

Challenge yourself introspectively:

- Are you being an inclusive leader? What does that term actually mean to you?
- Are you hiring people who are not just like you? In what ways are they different?
- Are you hiring people who remind you of you? In what ways are they similar?
- Who have you hired that is not just like you? For what roles? What levels? How often?
- Are you encouraging not just diversity in look and background but also diversity of thought?
- Has there been anyone that you think didn't fit a role? Why exactly didn't they?

- Are you looking at people's strengths versus how they make you feel?
- What causes you the most discomfort when you have to hire or select people for key roles or projects?

Your answers may surprise you; your answers may evolve over time. But whatever you do, challenge yourself to turn the noise into music.

DEI: THE OUTCOME

Let's go back to the idea that DEI in your organization is an outcome and not an input variable. Let's say that you are trying to lose weight, so you have to do some things differently. You eat healthier, you exercise more, and you change your daily routine. You change how you think about eating and your relationship with food. The outcome of those behaviors is weight loss. Now, consider a scenario in which weight loss occurred inexplicably, without making conscious changes or without an awareness of why it was happening. Then, weight loss is an input. You go to your doctor, where they treat your weight loss as a symptom of a problem and try to diagnose what is happening in your body because something might need to be corrected; either way, they need to evaluate what is causing the unexpected issue. Here, I want you to think of diversity as that weight loss outcome. There's a series of behaviors and actions that organizations need to take and be responsible for, and DEI should be a natural outcome of those actions. DEI should be one of the consequences of a broader set of strategic inputs. If DEI just seems to happen when there is no organizational effort at all, it might not be real, it might be a short-term gain, or it might be a sign of something else that is happening that, in the long term, might prove to be unsustainable. Now, don't get me wrong—the ideal long-term goal of any DEI program is that DEI itself becomes an integral part of the organizational DNA and feels effortless. But even then, it will still be a product of systematic mechanisms put in place to allow it to sustain successfully over time.

DEI naturally evolves from policies and processes that impact your employee experience in a globally positive way. If you think strategically about what helps your organization attract and retain talent, I can promise you that DEI will become the natural outcome of these strategic actions. Think about implementing proper remote-work strategies, for instance. A lot of organizational leaders fail to recognize that employees who identify as people with a disability are much better accommodated through remote work. Remember these people? You once told them that their disabilities or different abilities could not be accommodated. Then, COVID-19 came and proved you wrong. Now, you've expanded your workforce by including people who could have been doing the work and doing it well all along. But you initially hadn't created the policies and processes or invested in the technology and resources needed to accommodate that segment of talent. Remote work, or, in the very least, flexible work arrangements, has flattened the playing field for skilled talent across the country that previously was bound by the four walls of an office. That's a difference in policy that has a demonstrable DEI and business impact.

Here is another example: when you create programs and policies that allow people to take time off and provide opportunities to focus on self-care and mental health, you are creating a more equitable and inclusive environment without putting a DEI label on them—and they do not need one. Wellness policies and programs focus on improving well-being and mental health and promoting a better work-life balance for all employees. These policies and programs are implicitly diverse; they are for everyone's benefit and can be used in ways that meet each employee's individual and intersectional needs. They are also implicitly inclusive and equitable. How? By virtue of the kind of policy or program. They provide equity for people who are more at risk of experiencing health and wellness disparities of both the economic and physiological kinds.

These are the choices that organizations have to make when making people decisions, particularly those that impact the employee experience as a whole. Centering people-related business decisions on the people part of the decision seems obvious, but I'm here to tell you that this is not done even close to enough in our current corporate environments.

DESIGN EVERYTHING INCLUSIVELY (DEI)

I offer you a new meaning of DEI: Design Everything Inclusively. The objective of making these conscious and strategic organizational choices has one main question to answer: how can I support this group better? And to get to the answer, you have to break down the elements of work design:

- How can I provide better technology?
- How can I provide more mobile technology?
- How can I help people get together in different ways?
- How can I be creative?
- How can I think about mental health?
- How can I think about well-being?
- How do I think about work-life balance?
- How do I think about flexibility?

When you really put that time and work in, it's a beautiful outcome. You naturally get a better pipeline of people, more diverse people who recognize the impact of your policies on their employee experience. You will naturally keep your diverse talent. You will naturally keep *all* your talent. You will naturally earn a better external employer brand reputation. You will naturally shine in that diversity, in that inclusion, in that sense of equity.

Now, I'm not saying to discard initiatives that are specifically labeled DEI. Do. Not. Do. That. I repeat,

Do.

Not.

Do.

That.

Historically, we are organizationally and institutionally too far behind, and we have far too much of a gap to fill with these programs before we can ever think that we have engrained anything related to DEI into our corporate DNA. On top of that, conceptually, diversity and its related definitions—legal and cultural—can evolve, and with them policies, programs, and processes. That said, moving away from performative actions as an organization means that you have to stop focusing on issues as specifically diverse or specifically inclusive. If you have a DEI problem at your organization, *you just have a problem.* You have an organizational problem in the same way that you would have a problem if your merchandising systems broke down. It is going to permeate your organization unless you take the initiative to fix it by looking at your processes, your policies, and your pipeline.

DEI is a consequence of what organizations do, but most of them attempt to solve it differently from any other issue. If your product was bad or stocks were down, or if you received negative customer feedback, you would invest time, money, skills, and talent to improve these things. You would change your processes, your pipeline, your vendors, your logistics—whatever it would take to strategically change the outcome. But then DEI issues come along, and there is typically an unbothered, half-baked effort to *kind of* address it (at best).

Take the typical corporate claim of inadequate diversity within the talent pool. Well, instead of making such an offensive (and annoying and untrue) generalization, maybe you need to look at the design of your recruitment efforts. Do your recruiters maintain a diverse network of talent to tap into? Do any of them exist within diverse spaces where they can source talent and code-switch in languages that you cannot? Are your recruiters willing to pronounce diverse names? Are your recruiters themselves diverse?

DEI is about designing everything in your employee experience for inclusion. If you start centering your organizational design based on people and the employee experience, you will not constantly forget the LGBTQIA+ community. You will not constantly forget people with different abilities. You will not constantly forget geographical diversity. You will not constantly forget neurodiversity. You will not constantly forget ideological diversity. You will not constantly forget gender diversity. You will not constantly forget ethnic diversity. You will not constantly forget religious diversity. You will not constantly forget cultural diversity. You will not constantly forget age diversity. You will not constantly forget generational diversity. You will not constantly forget economic diversity. You will not constantly forget parental diversity. You will not constantly forget linguistic diversity. You will not constantly forget any form of diversity in all of its nuances, subtlety, and brilliance and all the intersections in between—and if you do, you will be able to adapt, adjust, and evolve more easily and with agility.

If you really want to focus on making substantive and tangible DEI policies, reframe the way you think about it to see it as a strategic, employee-experience outcome. And I promise you, when you build a brilliant employee experience that goes beyond a month, a day, a festival, a pizza party, or a season, it will permeate your culture and your organization. Then and only then is when you've made a real change. Then, you have created an inclusive culture.

CHAPTER 13

I THINK I LOVE
TRANSFORMATIONS

If you lead an organization that is constantly in transformation, I have some advice for you. Land the plane. Just land it. You keep circling around the airport aimlessly and it is starting to affect your passengers. They are extremely confused, nervous, and downright frustrated. At any moment, they are going to strap on their parachutes and take the leap. Now, replace the plane with your organization and the passengers with your employees. They are watching as you continually circle the destination without arriving at it. This is all highly problematic, and I am about to tell you why.

You are not alone in this costly mistake. Far too many organizations continuously undergo transformations, be it growth, a digital transformation, a leadership transformation, a reputational transformation, or mergers and acquisitions. And I have found that during these periods of change, leaders are focused on infrastructure and finance, with little consideration for the impact on the employee experience. Most organizations place employees on the expense side of their balance sheet. Their impact on profits and income gets understated or ignored because it is not easily spotted from an A-to-B perspective. But the reality is that transformations are often difficult and have a severe impact on employees and, by extension, the employee experience. The instability caused by never-ending transformation efforts drives increased turnover, institutional knowledge loss, and even reputational damage. I'm here to tell you that ignoring the impact of transformations on the employee experience is actually costly to your organization and hurts your bottom line.

The success of a transformation requires the trust of employees. Think about a merger and an acquisition or any other type of restructuring. You are asking your employees to trust you as you make a variety of organizational changes, even while they are feeling insecure in their job and nervous about what's happening. They are rightfully concerned about whether they will have a job or whether their leaders are going to change. They are thinking about the organizational structures and even the company's reputation. It's an extremely difficult place for employees to be. Yet you are asking them to trust you while they are consistently doing and feeling all of the things. Put yourself in their shoes for a moment and recognize the challenge of what you're asking. It is hard for anyone to trust when they're surrounded by uncertainty, and it's even worse when there seems to be a loud silence and lack of transparency. The result can be detrimental, as rumors become truth and people's imaginations run wild, even creating trauma in some cases.

FOCUSING ON THE EMPLOYEE EXPERIENCE DURING TRANSFORMATION

Because the employee experience is a significant part of an organization's culture, one of the most important steps an organizational leader can take during times of transformation is deciding to remain up-front and transparent. They must recognize that the transformation is going to be hard and counter the negativity by providing as much information as possible, even to the point of overcommunicating when necessary. They also must be careful not to communicate in a way that makes employees feel that something is being hidden from them. While a lot of things that happen in a transformation are difficult to predict and often require as much confidentiality as possible, leaders can still operate in transparency with their employees. They can show empathy and give clear direction. Let your employees in on the journey of the transformation and what they should be doing. It is hard for them to continue their job while being told that everything is frozen or on a "go slow" status. During transformations, employees often wonder about everything from whether they will still have a job to where they will land when the dust settles. They also wonder if they will get a promotion or be laid off, even trying to picture what the company's future will look like. As a leader, you should make an effort to acknowledge the things happening in real time, including layoffs.

I've often heard organizational clients push back against my survey recommendations during transformations. They tell me that it is not a good time because they expect that the results will be negative. While that might be true, organizational transformation is actually a great time to survey your employees. You really need this valuable data, even if only to establish a baseline of your transformation and to see if your transformation efforts have worked. But pretending that you don't have a way to understand and empathize with how your employees feel is insulting at best.

Collecting data about the transformation and the sentiment related to the transformation does two things. One, it includes the employee experience, or at least a willingness to hear the employee experience, during such a potentially difficult period. Two, it also helps you understand how you may be able to frame your communication. Do not discount the voice of your employees during a transformation. The uncertainty of these times can lead to a lot of talent loss. And from what I've seen, heard, and observed with many organizations, those losses might have been avoidable had organizations made any effort to keep their critical talent. Truthfully, it's like any relationship. If I don't trust you and I don't think that you treat me with the utmost respect, I have options. Another company will absolutely come along to sweet-talk me and tell me what I would like to hear. This is why transparency is super important. Your best talent has options, and they are often the first to go. Allow me to scream that from the mountaintops in case you missed it: *your best talent has the most options!* Add to that the elements of stress and uncertainty, and you might as well escort them out the door. Transformation should not be a test of loyalty. It is only supposed to be an organizational change to improve the outcomes that an organization is trying to accomplish. Remember, transformations are moments that matter. Like any other moment within an organization, you might not be able to make a transformation easy on your employees, but you can make it more palatable by really listening.

Listening during a transformation gives you an opportunity to find out all kinds of valuable data, including ways to maintain or improve your organizational culture in the midst of change. It's important not to make assumptions. You may be undergoing a wonderful digital transformation and everybody's really happy because it's a part of the employee experience that they have begged you to improve. But in fixing that, you are also taking away that job security and that role clarity that they had. So they are feeling uncomfortable and unsafe. Those feelings are not easy to get over, especially when they feel like their organization did not have their back while asking for their commitment and loyalty.

You can ask about their feelings and sentiment about any of the many factors impacting the employee experience during a transformation, be it organizational structure, reputation, working area, flexibility, or anything else you want or need to know about.

Data is always rich, so you always want to catch it. And as we previously discussed, you want some open-text data because in a transformation, there are likely little pockets of things happening that you have no clue about. There may be some cause for concern or something that can be celebrated. You may not know you have a superstar who is really bringing your transformation to life, and you will not know until you ask the question. Even during times of transformation, don't be afraid to ask the questions. Let the data be your friend.

LAND THE PLANE

I would not be me without offering a potentially unpopular opinion, so here goes. A transformation must have an end date. Otherwise, it is not a transformation—it is an organizational failure. Before you get mad at me, hear me out. Transformations mean that an organization is trying to transform something, whether it's a departmental restructuring, a leadership change, a technology shift, or merger and acquisition growth. It's trying to evolve from plan A to plan B. Let's go back to elementary school, where our teachers first explained the concept of transformation. We learned that a caterpillar transforms into a butterfly. But if that caterpillar goes into its cocoon and never comes out, it did not transform into anything. That is not a transformation. It is just a caterpillar going into a cocoon for a long nap.

The biggest complaint I hear about transformations when speaking with organizational leaders and employees is that they never seem to end. Some of these changes have been going on for years, and the plane still has not landed. Not only is it unfair and stressful for employees, but it also keeps leaders from seeing the full picture. They no longer recognize where point A, point B, or point C even lie anymore. It's very difficult to exist in a reality like that. This is why perpetual transformation is an organizational failure. Both leadership and employees end up existing in a state of what feels like constant chaos.

Many organizations want to transform to be more competitive or to try something new, which is fantastic because you want to constantly push the boundaries. But there must be a point where you stop and wonder, "Is this worth it? Did we learn anything? Do we know where we're going? Did we need to pivot and be transparent about that?" If you are not getting to something, you've got to pause and really reassess whether the strategy that you have implemented is working. A lot of companies had to end up doing that in the post-pandemic period. They had to pause and reassess where they were in terms of their strategies and transformations, which is a good thing. Sometimes it's okay not to double down on it because transformation is tough. Leading a transformation takes a lot of effort and it can take a lot out of you, so why wouldn't it take a toll on the actual organization? It creates not just stress on your employees but also stress within your organization. A lot of reputational damage can come from a poorly executed transformation or a transformation that is perpetual—and it's often not worth it.

When you're building out a transformation strategy, it is vital to build in agility and reassessment points. You have to figure out whether things make sense. You have to be real with yourself as a leader. You have to determine whether you need to pivot, and you have to set an end point. Otherwise, like I said before, you don't have a transformation—you have chaos.

It probably goes without saying that chaos is not good for the employee experience. So the longer your transformation effort goes, the more likely you are to start losing talent. Even some of your mid-tier talent that could go either way will start measuring their desire to leave. They will get to a point where the impact is too much. But even those that decide to stay will be constantly trying to figure out where they will fall and land. I have seen many cases in which transformations don't end well for the people who stuck with the organization. Just imagine that your accountant informed you that you would not get your check on time because they were in the middle of a transformation. I am willing to bet that you would not be a fan of that transformation. Well, that's how it feels to a lot of your employees.

TRANSFORM WITH INTENTION

A lot of organizations have been going through transformations in recent years, and, I can't state this enough, it is important to put that in the context of the employee experience in ways that are often overlooked. If you are a leader who is committed to what the employee experience should look and feel like, and you want to build or maintain a culture that reflects those goals, you must act intentionally in your transformation efforts. If you are starting with no end—or even an estimation of an end—in sight, then you are not planning a transformation at all. You are entering a period of change for change's sake and will get all the problems that come with that. Recognize that the longer it takes for an end to come into view, the more likely you are to harm your organization, trauma-tize your employees, and upend what might be positive about your employee experience.

And at the end of the day, once you get to a point where the transformation is not clearly ending, then it's no longer a transfor-mation, so you can stop calling it that.

CHAPTER 14

I THINK I LOVE
THE EVOLUTION
OF LEADERSHIP

As we think through how we evolve, disrupt, and even revolutionize the approach to building an employee-experience strategy,
it is important to understand how critical roles within the business
have to also change. Historically, when we think about C-suite executives, we think about overall operations and finance and how that is
all tied to strategic business outcomes. While the role of the chief HR
officer, especially within the tech industry, exists within the C-suite, it
has not necessarily been viewed as a strategic operations role. This is
primarily because, as discussed earlier in this book, this role oversees
employees who are not traditionally viewed as revenue-generating
entities within the organization, but rather employees viewed more
as depreciable liabilities that exist on the wrong side of the financial
balance sheet. As a result, when things get tough for the organization,
these employees are more often than not the first commodity that is
off-loaded. As such, the CHRO's role is viewed as the head people

manager and strategic organizer of people-related transactions and operations that serve as a functional yet expensive necessity for day-to-day interactions with the actual revenue-generating products and services the organization offers to consumers. Employees are viewed typically as a functional necessity until there can be a cheaper alternative, which often leans toward offshoring and replacement with technology when possible.

I know, it doesn't sound great when I describe employees this way or the manner in which I describe the perception of the CHRO role—but if there's one thing I have promised in this book, it is to be plain and straightforward. It's the only way to understand where we are today and how far we may need to go. But there is good news. The tides are shifting, and one good thing that emerged from the pandemic period of the early 2020s is that employee health and well-being came to the forefront, and many organizations had to admit that maybe, just maybe, employees were people and not simply the necessary evils needed to produce revenue-generating consumer goods and services. In addition, employees themselves, particularly those of younger generations, are viewing their own mental health and work-life balance with more priority and demanding more humanity from organizations. And they are willing to fight for and be uncompromising about these priorities in broader, more sweeping ways that have not been seen for at least maybe two generations. As a result, the roles of many executive leaders have to evolve as the employee experience is becoming a greater strategic priority, and no job is being pushed more into an immediate transformation as that of the CHRO.

THE CHRO

HR has always been deemed necessary, but up until recently, it has never been sexy. It was the bread at the buffet. Yes, you want it, and you are mad when it runs out, but the bread is not what got you to put on your elastic-waist pants and go out to the buffet. But in 2020, HR became the main course. Suddenly, it had main-character energy, pushing a lot of people into the spotlight. The days of CHROs keeping their heads down disappeared overnight. They had a spotlight on them because the entire organization needed everything from HR. Every decision, from innovation and technology to location strategy, required a CHRO to be in the room because it all had to center around employee wellness and health.

Others at the C-suite table used to see the CHRO as a supporting partner (and even an observer at times), but the CHRO quickly became the person at the table that everybody looked to for answers. While some of them took the opportunity to shine, others were not able to deal with the overnight transition. It was unfair because they should have always had that level of prestige at the table. They were suddenly being asked to make (quite literally) life-or-death decisions. HR turnover grew significantly during the pandemic because a lot of people were content being the bread. Now, they were expected to be the steak, and some just were not ready for that. They were being asked to deal with data operations and logistics in addition to the transactions, processes, and delegations their roles had been typically positioned around.

The pandemic era has left us in a weird stage, with a workforce that has shifted significantly, thanks in part to the Great Resignation and quiet quitting (or whatever other foolishness that consultants decided to sell us as a social media hashtag) but also to the natural progression of the time pre-2020. A significant population of workers died, and the remaining employees in the workforce were two to three years older than they were pre-pandemic. Students also graduated into a remote workforce during this time, which gave them a different perspective about work. And populations of people with disabilities or different abilities finally had their accommodations met after decades of being disregarded. Employees now have more awareness of mental health, and they feel empowered to demand what they need. With all these workforce changes, CHROs cannot afford to revert back to being the bread. They must speak up for the employee experience. They must understand data and people analytics in ways that they didn't understand before. They must grasp the impact of the employee experience in ways they did not have to fully comprehend before. They must recognize how every decision they make impacts how people are experiencing work. CHROs can no longer just look at their attrition numbers and say, "Well, this is what it is." They can't just look at a survey and say, "Well, this is our survey." A successful CHRO has to understand operations, technology, data, and the full context and nuances of the humans within their charge. They know they must truly look past the traditionally transactional nature of HR and better understand the complexities of those employees they lead. Having employee relations is not enough. CHROs must also communicate it because people are looking at them differently than they did before and with an expectation of a broader scope of decision-making capabilities and accountability.

CHROs have to be better at how they approach the concepts of DEI in the current working environment. The responsibility cannot be passed off to a chief diversity officer. It also cannot be reduced to a function of hiring some diverse individuals, creating some empty diversity programs, and/or starting some employee resource or affinity groups. CHROs must be more cognizant of broader employment, cultural, and geographical issues as well as legal and ethical concerns, such as continually evolving global privacy and AI laws. CHROs also have to consider the geopolitical landscapes in which their organizations exist. For example, they need to monitor how their employees are impacted by global interruptions, like endemics, pandemics, civil unrest, and threats of warfare, and they need to be able to have a point of view on how the organization can support any affected employees. They also need to advise more on if the organization should choose to take a stance on global issues and how this should be communicated back to the employees in an inclusive way. Additionally, in changing and chaotic economic environments where layoffs have become more of a strategy than a last resort, CHROs have to balance the transparent messaging with the humanity of these life-altering decisions for those affected and those who remain, walking a line that can be very tenuous even in the most optimal of circumstances.

There's a new element of courage that must come with being a CHRO. These professionals must be prepared to walk away from roles in which their voices are no longer being heard or where their talents are not being used effectively. There is need for a mix of confidence, vulnerability, empathy, and relatability, coupled with extreme business and data savvy, that has become crucial for stand-out CHROs. There is no longer any real opportunity for blending in or just getting by while serving as the conductor of an operational or transactional function. CHROs have become the prima ballerinas, the people to whom all eyes are on—including those of their peers and company boards—in a much more tacit way. And they should be. It should have always been this way. The higher standard should have always been present, as their responsibility is to a network of connected humans, and their decisions echo through each and every person's life under their stewardship. The burden should be heavy but fulfilling, and the CHRO role should not be for the faint of heart but for those who are strong in their resolve and commitment to their people and the employee experience. During the pandemic era, people looked to the CHRO for information, transformation, and inspiration. As further evidence, I am even seeing clear differences in how some academic training programs are repositioning HR responsibilities. And let's be clear, there will be another huge challenge. It might not be COVID-19, but it will be something (just ask any exhausted millennial). Employees are wired now to expect the next big catastrophe, and they will be looking to CHROs for answers. The new CHRO role is here to stay.

Here are some other roles that are evolving or need to evolve to keep up with the changing definitions of work, how we work, and the growing importance of sound employee-experience strategies.

HR BUSINESS PARTNERS

The HR business partner sometimes referred to as the people partner, has historically been the person who serves as a senior liaison generalist between HR and the actual business operation units. They tend to serve as a de facto head of HR, supporting designated executive leaders with policy and process execution along with the execution of key talent management activities. But we are seeing an inevitable shift and a broadening of the definitions of this role. It's no longer just about having a Society for Human Resource Management certification or generalist experience. It's also about having critical specialist skills that can elevate the functional employe experience strategy, such as experience with data analytics and insight generation. The HR business partner is now the person who has to build a fully functional business-level employee experience strategy and focus on measures, key performance indicators, and trends to better tell data stories from which business leaders can come to data-driven decisions. While their more day-to-day transactional generalist activities are not really shifting, the need to upskill in people analytics, product development, and end-to-end employee-experience management (including more emerging focus areas, such as wellness, work-life balance, work flexibility, location strategy, and work design) is becoming critical for this role.

I've even seen some businesses change the role name to people experience partner because they understand that HR can no longer be an entity separate from the rest of the organization. It all comes down to the employee experience that the organization is trying to provide and how the investment in that experience can be well supported and maintained sustainably in the long term and in ways that were not necessarily common before.

THE OTHER C-SUITE MEMBERS

From the C-suite perspective, these evolving roles are really centering around how other executives view HR as a function and how they develop a strategy and make decisions centered on the employee. Typical C-suite roles include the chief operating officer (COO), chief revenue officer, chief financial officer (CFO), and CEO (note that the chief diversity officer (CDO) will be discussed separately in the next section). These leaders are at a point where they have to rethink and recenter their investments to include how they see their employees—whether they want to or not. C-suite leaders must start thinking about their people in terms of longer-term investment as opposed to simply a return on investment per head. Like other investments, employees have to be assessed through not only cost per hire but also impact per role, legal issues due to mishandled employment decisions, the maintenance cost of experience management, and business risk to the employer value proposition (EVP). As many companies have found out, at least as of the 2020s, the talent attrition risk was greater than anticipated because leaders at the C-suite level are not reading the room and are pushing to fight back and revert the workforce position to what it was in 2018; it isn't working. The shifting tide will drag those who are unaware and unprepared away with it.

We've seen companies generously invest billions into investments that are . . . well . . . questionable at times, such as an online universe where avatars have no legs (at least as of this writing—here's to the hope for legs one day!). If you spend billions on what may be deemed as ill-advised investments that do not go as planned and then you turn around and lay off hundreds or thousands of people at the first sign of trouble, how does one make sense of that? The stark reality is that many of the reasons companies had layoffs in the 2020s were not surprising upon close examination, like unnecessary over-hiring and focusing on total revenue rather than profit margins to measure growth—things that were in no way sustainable business practices.

These layoffs and related employee experience conundrums were the product of bad executive decisions based on bad fore-casting, bad judgment, bad consulting, and yes, greed—the chase for constant growth in shareholder value even in economic down-shifts. Bad decisions made at the leadership level disproportionately affected employees, especially those at the most vulnerable levels. You are making a bolder statement about how you see your own people than failed investments in nonessential product spend or, say, the lack of accountability for bad business decisions. Your laid-off employees are not the only ones seeing these bad decisions or being impacted by it—so are the ones who remain, so is the poten-tial talent you may want later, so are customers, and so are members of the general public at large. And yes, in the short term, you may not see the damage, but in the long term—as long as you are there and your leadership remains intact and unscathed from the conse-quences of executive decisions—the virus of toxicity will systemat-ically embed itself into your company culture. And fixing that is so much harder than breaking it.

This is why I believe that a lot of C-suite leaders still don't nec-essarily see their employees as people. They can easily see their customers that way but often struggle to not commodify their employees. They need to alter their mindsets so that they see the employee experience as a product and their employees as key stakeholders for and customers of that product. Yes, we know that people cost money. We've always known that, but how do you invest in such a way that you can get the maximum return on investment that you're looking for? Because if you're not investing, why are you calculating a return? If you aren't putting money into the stock market, why are you checking to see how much money your stock made? Why are you checking the lottery numbers if you never purchased a ticket? Yet this is what a lot of leaders do when it comes to their own employees.

Providing a salary is not an organizational investment. A salary is a fair-exchange business transaction. It is the contractual value that you place on a person's role and the expected outcomes and impact of the agreed-upon work. If you want to maximize the return, you need to invest more. CFOs, CEOs, COOs, chief revenue officers, and chief product officers have no problem investing in all other aspects of their organizations. The chief product officer will add whatever necessary to ensure that a new product makes an impact. Chief marketing officers have shifted entire marketing campaigns to get better feedback, have greater impact, and get better product attention. Why are so many C-suite leaders willing to invest in everything except their employees? Because they have this mindset that they are paying a salary (and, in some cases, benefits and bonuses) for the person to do the job, which should be enough for the person to work hard. Yet they do nothing to optimize this so-called investment through a proper employee-experience strategy. They will invest more to get more returns out of everything— except their employees. Let me be clear. An operational business plan with no employee experience strategy is incomplete. Period. And it's insane to me in this present moment of change, and with so many lessons from the pandemic and post-pandemic period, that many executive leaders still haven't figured this out. Or maybe they still just don't care.

THE CHIEF DIVERSITY OFFICER (CDO)

The role of the CDO has gotten a lot more attention in recent years (meaning in the early 2020s), but in actuality, the CDO's ultimate role should be to work themselves out of a job. Will it happen? Probably not, because people will always participate in foolishness, but that should be the goal. Here is the thing: Diversity within your organization should not be limited to being an HR issue. It is an operational issue that should span multiple elements of how the business functions, including vendors and suppliers.

Diversity is a factor that can enhance all elements of innovation and reach within your organization, which can pay dividends for the revenue-generating products and services that your organization creates. It's not an HR issue when you are diversifying your products or strategizing your marketing. It is not an HR issue when you're trying to increase sales or your revenue stream. The role of the CDO in its most effective iteration should be akin to that of the COO. But here is the reality: many CDOs are hired as performative, check-the-box placeholders, set up to fail by being given limited resources and a narrow scope for operational oversight. They are often relegated to working with HR and creating activities, programs, and groups in a way that feels fragmented and ineffective. In short, many CDOs are set up to fail. And it doesn't take them long to recognize this and burn out or become disillusioned (or both), as data has shown that the average CDO tenure tends to be two to three years. One of the biggest issues is that CDOs are brought in to be reactive rather than proactive and strategic. When larger-scale social and civil issues arise, as they tend to do in fits and starts, they are often yo-yoed in and out the spotlight with fluctuating levels of resources and support. You can't just keep putting someone in the role with zero investment. It's essentially a show so that your company can say, "At least we have a CDO."

Unfortunately, for a lot of CDOs, burnout is high because they are being asked to solve centuries' worth of institutional imbalances with little to no real budget, infrastructure, or other resources. They have nothing more than a wish, a dream, the audacity of hope, and a prayer (and, you know, folks love to give them thoughts and prayers). Then, you also ask them to go into organizations and form employee resource groups or affinity groups, where they are tasked with asking underrepresented and historically marginalized groups to solve their own problems . . . for free. What an absolutely awful employee experience for these CDOs!

The CDO should not only be somebody who is passionate about diversity but also someone who understands data, which is something that has been missing from the role's core requirements. CDOs should be able to get to the heart of the broken rungs, gaps, and equity analyses using data to support their action plans. Now, I'm not saying that the CDO should be a data analyst, but they should be given the budget to get continuous support so that they can always monitor overall organizational data in a more comprehensive and tactical way, and they should be able to advise their peers and other organizational leaders on their own gaps and strategic action plans.

Speaking of data, as a whole, organizations need to do a much better job of reporting on inclusion and diversity analytics, and they can do this by ensuring that they are producing robust predictive models that can provide guidance on real action and growth in ways that help the company's strategic and bottom-line goals.

Here is the bottom line: The current CDO model is simply not sustainable, and guess what? It was never meant to be. I remind leaders all the time that people—and by "people," I mean their employees—are not stupid. And the employee segments they think they're placating aren't daft either. They completely know what is happening. And the ones who really can't take it will leave—including the talented ones, to be clear. It shouldn't be a show. If you want a show, go to Hollywood. If you want real results, get into strategy. It's high time that companies decide and be honest about what they really want. If you don't care about DEI, don't keep wasting everyone's time. The only people who executives are fooling with an impotent CDO position are maybe themselves. And let's be clear, many of the people who come into these roles are brilliant and tactical and deserve so much better.

PEOPLE-CENTERED LEADERSHIP AND YOUR LVP

In this book, I have talked a lot about people-centered design within the context of the employee experience, but what does that mean for the evolution of leadership? Here is the thing—leadership doesn't have to merely be a positional status that is steeped in transaction, control, and power. It is beyond descriptive characterizations such as transactional, empathetic, charismatic, and transformational. Leadership is an action. Leadership is a legacy. Leadership reflects the totality of the way you execute the objectives assigned to your role, the influence you carry, and the impact that you have on the people and the culture that you are charged with developing and nurturing. You are not a leader if there is nobody to lead. With this in mind, I challenge all people leaders to take the time to create an annual leadership value proposition (LVP).

The LVP typically answers the question *What do I offer as a leader that sets me apart?* Many leaders tend to make LVPs that solely focus on their organizations, customers, and business results but not on their people and how they plan to effectively lead those people. In redesigning and people-centering how we think about leadership, the focus of the LVP needs to shift. An LVP should answer the question *Why should I be led by you?*

Creating an LVP should focus on the following:

- What do you offer as a leader that sets you apart?
- What values and beliefs do you hold that drive your behaviors?
- What is your vision for the future of your team?
- What do the people for whom you are responsible need from you?
- Why should anyone want to be led by you?

All this means is that more effective and people-centric leadership requires that leaders have to be better at listening. Once again, I recognize that listening to employees may be uncomfortable at times for leaders, but it is a non-negotiable and crucial element of effective and successful leadership. The bottom line? Listening makes leaders more effective, and effective leaders make the employee experience much, much better.

THE EMPLOYEE EXPERIENCE LINK

I want you to finish this chapter with the understanding that all these roles, whether you want to believe it or not, are inextricably linked to the employee experience as a product, and you need to keep this fact in mind as you make critical organizational decisions. Once you start making more people-centered decisions, the employee experience will be a natural product that comes from them. It may take time to build the infrastructure for sustainability, but it will help with all elements of talent planning as well as leadership and development. In short, it will jump-start your employer value proposition (EVP) and whatever your organizational culture aspirations are (i.e., your culture North Stars).

CHAPTER 15

I THINK I LOVE EXITS

A word about exits before I exit (see what I did there?). I cannot write a book about the employee experience without talking about employee exits. In fact, in my experience, responding to unexpectedly high attrition rates, especially those of desirable or key talent, is usually the catalyst for organizational leaders and decision makers to give the employee-experience strategy a second look. First thing's first, I want to make a distinction between the types of exits I will be discussing: voluntary and involuntary.

TYPES OF EXITS

A **voluntary exit** is where an employee initiates the exit, be it with a traditional notice period or an impulsive "I quit"; the key is that the exit is primarily driven by the employee. In some cases, an employee's exit may be based on a mutual agreement between the employer and employee. This is common during mergers and acquisitions, layoffs, and restructurings that create potential foreseeable redundancies. An exit may also come through an offer, such as early retirement. These kinds of aforementioned exits are still deemed voluntary because the employee is actively involved in discussions and usually has the ability to make choices about their transition and exit process. This chapter will lean heavily on voluntary attrition in discussing exits. There is more existing data and practice around voluntary exits and typically fewer legal issues surrounding them, causing it to be a less sensitive topic and way to leave an organization.

In many cases, an employee does not simply leave an organization because they do not like it. Instead, they realize that there is no room left to grow. Moving through any organization can feel like a triangle with only so much room for advancement. Many people find out the hard way that simply keeping your head down, working hard, and delivering results—the myth of meritocracy—is not enough to help them get better opportunities or even compensation. The only option for most employees might be to exit (and maybe come back). It's a strategic career decision that is sometimes necessary when the only way to increase woefully inadequate pay is to exit the company and return after a year or two, when you can then level into the right salary. Unfortunately, there is also a corporate reality at work in which it is often easier to get properly compensated as an external candidate than as an internal candidate.

This issue is even more pertinent for underrepresented and historically marginalized groups, where representation at higher levels is more important because direct sponsorship and advocacy play such a big part in these groups' ability to move up through the organizational ranks. When trying to move up the corporate ladder, these employee segments often find that rungs are broken and that there are no steps they can take to go farther up.

Here is a secret: nobody really *wants* to exit an organization, not even the people who have been labeled as job hoppers for moving around a lot in their careers. Organizations must begin to recognize these movements as more of an indication of the companies that these people have been employed with as opposed to a testament to the person's character, performance, or professionalism. Here's the thing: some people just have a lower tolerance for the nonsense that occurs within a workplace, and when the economy is doing well, these same employees often have more options to exercise. They have decided that their company does not have a positive work environment, and they do not have to stay.

Exiting can be traumatic, even when it is voluntary. It is a major moment that makes a lot of people feel like they are losing or grieving a part of themselves and their identities, especially if it was a job (or company) that they truly felt connected to. Sometimes, it is not the job they are leaving, but the organization. It is not the people they are leaving, but the culture. Exiting employees are often grieving one aspect of exiting (like coworkers and work besties) while simultaneously recognizing that it is what they have to do for their own career goals, personal needs, quality of life, mental health, or well-being (or any combinations of these). Unfortunately, when employees make the decision to leave and put in their notice, they often face retribution and retaliation. But that never makes sense. If an employee decides to leave, especially your talented employees or high performers, yes, you might be disappointed, but what good is it at that point to make their lives harder? Let them go, and give them a soft landing rather than a shove. If you are a leader or people manager, take my advice here—don't try to force people into staying at jobs that they do not want to do anymore, even if you feel disappointed or slighted. That never ends well for anyone. Take the loss, learn the lesson, do better.

Involuntary exits are exits that are initiated by the employer, and the employee tends to have little to no control over or say in how it happens or what the exit process or transition entails. Typical forms of involuntary exits are performance-based firing and layoffs due to reductions in force, restructurings, cost savings, strategy pivots, or job redundancies. According to the US Department of Labor, there were 15.4 million layoffs in the United States in 2022, with 6.9 million layoffs between August and December 2022. There were just over 168,000 layoffs between January and June 2023. Additionally, 40 percent of Americans have been laid off or terminated from a job at least once in their lifetimes, with many people, across all industries, reporting multiple layoffs over a one-year period between 2020 and 2023 (and that includes me, who, in fact, had two layoffs in one twelve-month period between July 2022 and July 2023!). Involuntary terminations are usually sensitive to discuss and measure given the general abruptness of it, the legal risk around it due to potential legal recourse, and the potential ethical issues surrounding the decision to let someone go. They are also extremely interruptive to the employee's life and livelihood and, in all honesty, can create serious economic hardships and professional repercussions for that person as they attempt to move on from it.

Involuntary exits can be extremely traumatic, not just to the person being forced to exit but also to those who have to stay in the role afterward. Involuntary turnover, especially in the form of mass layoffs, can be destructive to company cultures due to a serious erosion of trust, and it can devastate innovation and progress due to institutional knowledge loss and reluctance—on the part of those who are retained—to take risks for fear of also being let go. There is also evidence that big periods of involuntary exits tend to be followed by a spike in voluntary exits within the six months following the involuntary exit event (all economic variables being relatively stable, of course).

EXITS AND THE EMPLOYEE EXPERIENCE

Now that we have a better grasp on these two types of exits, let's back up a bit to discuss why people actually leave their jobs. We know that the top reasons that people leave jobs are to get away from specific managers; for better career opportunities; for better salaries; for better benefits, including quality of life and flexibility; and due to their distrust of company leaders (or, by extension, their lack of faith in the company direction). But what is it about these factors that motivates people to decide that they have had enough and exit a company, one they have worked hard for and loved? What is it that underpins and finally spurs that drive to move on? On the surface, it's easy to say that it's just the job, or just a bad manager, or just the money, or even just the company. In many cases, people who exit cannot eloquently articulate the core reason why, but they just feel like they have to. And don't bother to check data from the average organizational exit survey or exit interview process. Those are usually too generic and badly written to get robust data. In addition, the timing or process for most exit surveys or interviews often feel too precarious for the exiting employee to be comfortable with being totally honest. I'm here to tell you that the answer tends to lie deeper than those surface-level reasons.

What is it about the job? Is it the lack of role clarity? Overwork? Unreasonable expectations? A skills mismatch? Did the job change from the one the employee was hired to do?

What is it about the manager? Do they not give feedback? Are they bullying? Are they biased? Are they untrained? Are they themselves too overworked to manage people well? Do they micromanage? Do they create unnecessary conflicts?

What is it about the company leaders or company direction? Is the leadership insensitive or abusive? Does it foster a culture that promotes unethical behavior? Is the company strategy unclear? Is the company getting bad press? Do the leaders not communicate changes well?

I can go on and on about things like this, but to understand how the employee experience is correlated with exits, we have to go much, much deeper. We have to find out what is broken and where the gaps are. We also have to call a crucial result of a poor employee experience what it is: workplace trauma.

WORKPLACE TRAUMA

Workplace trauma is the result of abuse, stress, and burnout within an organizational context. Though we have reached a point of better understanding how trauma in one area of life can affect us in multiple aspects of our lives, we have been trained to believe that we are supposed to be superhuman when it relates to work. Regardless of what negativity we experience in the workplace, we are typically expected to just get over it and see it through, usually in an effort to get a chance, however remote, to be promoted or grow at the organization in question. These expectations are followed so that, as an employee, you don't get seen as a complainer, or weak, or as a problem. But here is the thing about workplace trauma: it is a real and palpable thing regardless of whether it was a toxic or an abusive work situation or just a really bad breakup with an otherwise pleasant work environment. This trauma happens slowly over time, continues to build—with employees long past stress, long past burnout—and feeds on the resulting brokenness.

Workplace trauma can make people question their whole careers and professional selves. Historically, people have been conditioned to embed work in their lives, not just as simply something they do but as a key part of their whole identities. But when it comes to workplace trauma, people typically have not been trained to recognize or acknowledge it as a real thing, and, in general, most people are not in a position where they have the privilege to give themselves the security, space, and time between jobs to recover from or unlearn bad practices. This means that they are constantly carrying trauma from job to job and from company to company. And many people who are carrying these traumas are moving into leadership positions and are unintentionally inflicting the trauma on others, who will then likely take that with them to the next job and company. Breaking the cycle might seem impossible, but acknowledgment is half the battle. Intentionally designing brilliant employee experiences that nourish strong cultures can go a long way in healing broken employees and our historically broken corporate culture.

The impact of workplace trauma on underrepresented and historically marginalized groups is also far worse because they are dealing with it on top of many other social, generational, and institutional traumas on a day-to-day basis. But then they are also typically told not to talk about or even acknowledge any kind of workplace trauma because that would be unprofessional. They are constantly given the message that burning any professional bridge, even the most terrible ones, can have catastrophic consequences for their careers. Meanwhile—and let me say this clearly—some bridges are meant to be burned. Accountability lives in that fire.

Workplace trauma is borne by cultures with undisputed forms of workplace hazing, with the mentality of "I went through it, and I survived just fine, so you should go through it, too." But when you look back on those negative experiences, were they really good for you? If you could have been elevated without being abused by a manager or mistreated during the performance management process, wouldn't that have been better? What about the times they silenced your innovative ideas, or you were emotionally beaten down to the point of complete burnout and submission at work. If you could have been elevated without those traumas, wouldn't that also have been better?

Here is the thing, we generally don't treat the relationships and experiences that people have at work and with their jobs in the same way we treat other relationships, and it is quite absurd. Nobody tells someone to stay in an abusive relationship, but we directly and indirectly tell employees to do that all the time regardless of the experience they are having in the workplace. We excuse the trauma as an acceptable trade-off for the opportunity of working with the company. We must break out of that habit. It holds neither the organizations nor their leaders accountable for their unacceptable actions.

Amid the continuing mass layoffs, particularly across the tech industry, at the time of this writing in 2024, I have seen people laid off in the most disrespectful and painful ways. They suddenly lost a massive part of their identities and who they believed their companies to be. Yet their LinkedIn headlines are filled with "ex-this company" and "ex-that company." If you were in a relationship and your significant other dumped you in a painful and traumatic way, would you go on a dating site and call yourself "Bob's ex-girlfriend" or "Randy's ex-boyfriend" or "Sherry's ex-partner?" Would you label yourself as such? No, you would not. So why do you do that in your professional life? In fact, some of you need to change those headlines to "survivor of this company or that company." Our work is so tied into our identities that, even after being traumatized, we use it as a beacon of who we are.

We are so indoctrinated in the notion of making corporations happy (with whatever their definition of professionalism is) that we end up perpetuating the trauma instead of putting ourselves in the position to help other people avoid that trauma. Leaders that move from one position or company to another don't take the time to work through the trauma they endured to get into their positions. They simply move on and perpetuate the cycle in their treatment of their employees.

In a bit of good news, some companies have begun trying new and innovative ways of addressing the issue of workplace trauma and well-being by giving new hires a paid week before starting their new positions. These companies and their leaders seem to understand the value of letting employees take some time between roles to process their former experience before jumping into a new situation. Too often, organizations want people to be their most productive selves but are only willing to support their employees' broken selves at work. Make it make sense. It is a cycle that must be broken, and that starts with admitting the prevalence of workplace trauma and recognizing that it carries the same physical and mental effects of any other form of trauma.

Contrary to popular belief, people do not actually like to leave their jobs and organizations. People crave familiarity. People *want* a reason to stay at their current jobs. Having to do a job search is tedious, especially when the market is not at its best. If you do have workplace trauma, the entire process of applying, interviewing, and being rejected can be re-traumatizing with every step. And starting over in a new environment can be extremely stressful.

A QUIET EXIT

Exits are part of the employee experience, and organizations can absolutely give people a soft landing. I tell leaders that there is no good way to lay people off, but there are definitely terrible ways to do so. I have seen races to the bottom for no other reason than a lack of consideration for the employee experience. Whether voluntary or not, people are still employees when exiting, and, in some cases, they might come back as employees in the future.

We also need to stop shaming people into making work their whole identities and discourage them from rushing from one negative employee experience to another. Sometimes you just need to date the job or flirt with it for a bit. But you do not need to immediately get engaged and marry it. It is not a romantic movie, and we need to be more practical about how we view taking new jobs and our relationships with work. In some, or even many, cases, there may be a point where the best thing for everyone is the breakup between the employee and the job—and there is nothing that the organization can do about it. And that needs to be okay. We need to normalize this.

Offboarding does not have to be a traumatic or dismissive experience. It can be one where the working relationship ends respectfully and considerately, where maybe you will even find each other again one day. That's the way an exit should work. That is a quiet experience. Your organization has gained an alumnus—an ambassador. Right now, a lot of organizations' exit processes are broken and filled with the expectation that people should simply be grateful for having had a chance to be employed there. Nope.

The employee experience matters even until the employee's last day. Exits and how the offboarding process is designed, and how it can manifest in the organization's EVP, should be a critical part of any comprehensive employee-experience strategy.

CHAPTER 16

I THINK I LOVE SOLUTIONS

Now that you have come to the end of this book, you may be thinking, "I understand the employee experience, but now what do I do with all of this incredibly amazing and valuable information?" Well, those might not be your exact words, but just let me dream. I want you to consider this question in two ways. From the employer's perspective, what do I do as a leader to make the employee experience better? From the employee's perspective, how do I recognize that my experience is not meeting expectations, and what should I be looking for?

Before I give some actionable steps that you can take toward answering these questions, I want you to pat yourself on the back. You took a big step in and took the time to truly understand the facets of the employee experience. There are so many people who would not even get here, so thank you! (Also, thank you for reading this book!)

Now I want you to take a close look at three things. Your pipe-lines, your processes, and your policies, all of which feed into your programs. Let's start with the pipelines. Consider these questions:

- What is your talent pool?
- What type of people are you trying to attract?
- What type of people are currently in your culture?
- What is your objective?
- If you don't have the experience you hope to provide, who do you need to bring in to help you?
- In all the variations, manifestations, and intersections of diversity, who do you need to help you create the culture you are trying to build?

Remember that the employee experience is a product of your culture, which is a matter of people. You can try as much as you want to tell people what your vision for your culture, but your words mean nothing if the culture does not manifest at the level in which people are affected by your decisions. You also need to look at your pipeline. Ask questions about who is doing your sourcing and how their personal biases might be coming into play. Do you need to change the people that new and internal candidates primarily inter-act with to help you craft the type of culture you want to build?

I want you to consider your processes and how they affect everything from the time that someone applies for a job at the orga-nization to the time that they leave. Every process that you imple-ment is influenced by the experience and culture that you are trying to create. Every experience is driven by the candidate experience and is reinforced by every subsequent experience until they exit (in whatever form it takes: voluntary or involuntary). When you think about every one of your processes, you must consider inten-tionality and a people-centered design. Ask yourself, "How will making this decision affect this segment of people?" For example, if you think of onboarding as a process, what is the impact that you want the new employee to make in 30 days, in 90 days, in 180 days? What is the long-term impact that you expect from this person in this role?

A lot of leaders take the easy way out by saying things like "I want them in a role where they can develop." But what does that even mean? The key is to define the impact that you want and determine whether your processes are truly going to direct the employee to that expected outcome. If not, you are actively setting the employee up for failure. Your pipeline is the source of your talent, internally and externally. The experiences for both internal and external candidates should feel seamless and congruent, and the experiences should reflect the long-term expectations of the role, at least what was promised. If it does not, what are the roadblocks that you can remove, and what resources can you provide for improvement?

Let's take a look at your policies now. Policies influence everything that your organization does, so I want you to consider these questions:

- What roadblocks are your policies creating, as opposed to efficiencies?
- What biases are your policies creating?
- How are your policies affecting the pipeline that you are trying to build?
- How does your policy affect the culture that you hope to have and the implementation of that culture?

To reiterate, questioning and fleshing out your policies, pipelines, and processes are the core of a people-centered design, and they underpin new programs and investments needed to design and maintain a positive employee experience. Remember that your employee experience is a product, and your EVP is a promise to produce that product consistently for those who agree to work for you. This is a big part of what they are buying from you in exchange for working for you and getting a salary.

I KNOW I LOVE PEOPLE-CENTERED DESIGN

It all comes down to one lesson that I want you to learn from reading this book, working with me, and interacting with me: people-centered design. How does every process that you implement, every pipeline that you build, and every program that you create affect different groups of people? And how do you ensure the efficiency and success of those pipelines, processes, and policies? Do you focus on people when you design work? Is work designed to be a transaction or an experience?

From the very beginning, when you are breaking down a system and thinking about each of the elements, you should be designing for the people who will be impacted. And when you modify or update those systems, you should think about how the changes will impact those people and the experiences they are having as well as the culture that you are trying to build over the long term. A people-centered mindset needs to direct all elements of your strategy, all elements of your bottom line, and all elements of your operations. It directs all elements of the workplace life cycle, from the time employees come in, train, and onboard to when they undergo performance management or leave your organization.

I want you to think about how the decisions you make impact groups of people, particularly groups of people that you have not thought about before. How do they affect men, women, historically marginalized people and underrepresented groups, majority groups, different cultures, different geographies, different regions, different economic backgrounds, people with different abilities, people who are neurodivergent, parents, and so on? As you design, consider how adverse effects can be mitigated through the creation of an exception or a more inclusive design.

When you think about a people-centered design, and you really think about how you intentionally design every element of your system, then what you are doing is creating not just a culture but also all the byproducts that come along with it. You no longer have to put DEI, true inclusiveness, functional culture, and removing toxicity as input variables because they become embedded in every element of your decision and, by extension, the way you design work.

Don't worry. You don't have to do it all in one day. Just start with one policy, one process, one pipeline, or one program. For instance, focus on what happens when people apply to your organization. Improvements to that one area will start to evolve your employee experience into alignment with your employer value proposition. As a result, your leaders will also start to align with your culture in their leadership value proposition. Then, you create a functional, efficient culture that is tied into the business outcomes and experience outcomes that you have been looking for. It is really not that hard, but it takes intentionality.

And once you build it, you as a leader, or you as employee, can honestly say, **"I think I love my job."**

ABOUT THE AUTHOR

Kalifa Oliver, PhD, is an international experience coach, executive advisor, keynote speaker, author, and expert on building brilliant experiences using people-centered design and analytics. She has consulted for several companies and industries including tech startups, non-profits, and Fortune 500 companies to help them reposition their culture and employer value proposition with a focus on employee experience and people analytics. She is also a dynamic speaker who coaches leaders on reaching their leadership goals through taking control of their voice, space, and energy and through walking into their Main Character Season.

A native of Trinidad and Tobago, Dr. Oliver has her PhD in Industrial-Organizational Psychology from Clemson University and her Certification in People Analytics from Massachusetts Institute of Technology (MIT) and is a proud graduate of Benedict College, an HBCU in Columbia, South Carolina.

www.ingramcontent.com/pod-product-compliance
Lightning Source LLC
Chambersburg PA
CBHW030514210326
41597CB00013B/904

9 781953 315359